PREY

for

THE ENEMY

PREY

for

THE ENEMY

by

ANNIE APLIN

XULON PRESS

Xulon Press
2301 Lucien Way #415
Maitland, FL 32751
407.339.4217
www.xulonpress.com

Printed in the United States of America.

ISBN-13: 978-1-6312-9679-6

This book contains terrorizing events that happened before and after the murder of Billy Joe Aplin in Seadrift, Texas, on August 3, 1979. Following his death, regular phone calls to his parents, Mr. and Mrs. Aplin, from Vietnamese, shouting, "Five more to die! Five more to die!" Six months later, after several attempts on the lives of many United States citizens, came the tragic deaths of Billy Joe's sister, Josie, and her husband, Dale.

These horrific actions are what led Mr. and Mrs. Aplin—with their entire family—to abandon their homes and businesses in Seadrift, Texas, fleeing for their lives!

It leads one to ask, "When someone in the world is fleeing torture, terrorism, and murderous conditions, they come to America for protection and asylum, so where in the world do Americans flee when they are the ones needing protection and asylum?" We became refugees within our own country and . . .

PREY FOR THE ENEMY

DEDICATION

I dedicate this book in memory of my parents, B.T. and Sarah Aplin. Their love of God, family, and country was my guiding light. Their work ethic and sacrifice for their loved ones made an indelible impression on my life.

This book is also written in memory of six of my seven siblings, and to one living sister, Zonie, with love and gratitude. This book is dedicated to hope in the future of America and our posterity.

I want to thank my daughter, Angel, for naming the book, and for sacrificing our time while I worked.

I also dedicate this book to several nieces—Misty, Cheryl, Regina, Sharon, and Sonja—for helping with research on this project. Plus numerous friends for enduring my long work hours and unending questions. Thank you all!

My sincerest thanks to a dear friend, Gail Pelletier, who asked me to tell my family's story in 2001, and did an amazing job with the typesetting and keeping me on task. "Mahalo Nui Loa, Gail!"

This book is also dedicated to those who have suffered the same loss but have not had a voice until now.

It is my fervent prayer that this story will help provoke change in laws to prevent these travesties of justice from happening to anyone else in the future.

ENDORSEMENTS

The sudden, horrific, and tragic murder of my father being ripped out of my life was beyond devastating. His absence in our family unit created immeasurable tragedies that echo to this very day!

It is my dearest hope that good will come from the unnecessary loss of his life!

I pray this book will contribute to changing laws and practices surrounding the immigration of those looking to come to this great country of ours.

Dearly missing my father still.

—Cheryl Ann Aplin

It is a terrifying tragedy when a family is grounded in the truth and liberty of a country like America and then destroyed by the governmental leadership of that same country. I have known Annie for over twenty years, and I know the faithful endeavors this family has put forth to continue to be a part of fighting for the truth and liberty and freedom that America portrays. I believe this book will reveal an epiphany of truth to the reader as to how one person can make a difference in revealing lies, deception, and murder. I believe it will also bring healing to others who have experienced similar situations. Annie reveals the evil behind the decisions of some of our elected officials. This is an eye-opening read that should make a difference in our land.

—Charmaine Herlong,
life coach and author of *Gateway to Glory*

As a first-generation immigrant, I found this story of familial loss and ardent vocation for justice a harrowing account of Ms. Aplin's vehement pursuit for the truth. This amidst a backdrop of violation and why such travesties can turbulently rupture our lives. A must-read for all those burdened by the weight of loss and coming to terms with why.

—Steve Sloane,
author of *The Gaiety*

The first time I heard Annie tell her story, I knew she had to write a book. I had no idea these things were happening right here in the U.S., without consideration for a family so badly beaten down by invaders from another country. I am so glad she decided to write her story. Annie is one of the strongest women I have ever known. You can feel her pain as she writes the words on every page. The world needs to know the truth, and I highly recommend this book.

—Gail Pelletier

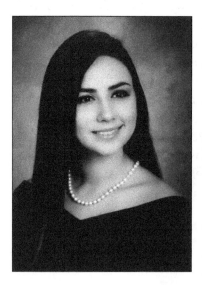

Kate Weaver is the great-great granddaughter of Mr. and Mrs. Aplin. She not only attends college but received more than fifty art awards in her junior high and high school years as well as recognition from the Georgia House of Representatives. In addition to being an amazing Christian Artist, she can work with any art media and design. I am grateful and privileged to work on this heart-wrenching project and cover design with my precious niece. Thank you, Kate!

—Annie Aplin,
author

TABLE OF CONTENTS

COTTON FIELDS BACK HOME

B illy Joe Aplin was one of eight children born into a farming family in Georgia. They were a typical country family, rising before the rooster crowed to the smell of their mother's homemade biscuits baking. Mrs. Aplin also had potatoes frying in the huge iron skillet to make biscuit and potato sandwiches for their lunch out in the fields while they were picking cotton.

This was *real country*. Mrs. Aplin wasn't cooking on an electric stove. It was a wood-fired range. Her iron was heated over the fire of the stove, and their home was heated by a huge fireplace, with wood chopped in the forest. The bathroom was lovingly called a "Johnny house" or an "outhouse" and was located outside, down a long, dusty, winter-cold trail. Mrs. Aplin washed her large family's laundry by boiling it in a huge three-legged iron wash pot. She then scrubbed it on a scrubbing board to ensure it was clean before rinsing and hanging it on a clothesline to dry. Later, clothes and bedsheets were sprinkled with water and ironed by the iron on the fire. When permanent press was invented, it was a welcome addition in the Aplin home!

Life was hard on the farm as Mr. and Mrs. Aplin loaded their eight children into the car to go into the fields to work. They hoed the rows of their crops to keep them free of weeds, picked cotton, and pulled and shook peanuts at harvest time. Whatever was required on the farm, the entire Aplin family did. No one was exempt from work, not even the youngest child, "Annie." It is this youngest child of eight writing and recounting our family's story.

L-R Front to Back: Rudy, Doc, neighbor friend, Noopy,

Mrs. Aplin, Annie, Aunt Ruth

When I was old enough to go into the fields, Mother would sew a work sack for me to pick cotton out of a huge flour sack. These flour sacks had beautiful prints and designs. They were filled with cooking flour, which was dumped into huge storage tins so Mother could use the colorful fabric. She was an amazing seamstress, and without pattern or machine, she would hand-stitch all of our clothes.

Until I was old enough to go into the fields and work, I could run free and play with the farm animals. Showing my artistic side, I would squeeze wild purple berries between my hands and fingerpaint on the wood walls of the hog pen. Then I would step back and look at it, beaming with pride at what I thought was a beautiful painting. I loved the farm! To this date, my best artistic work was done with berry juice on those hog pen walls.

When I was very young, my mother left my two-years-older sister, Margrette, and I at the end of the cotton row under a makeshift tent while she worked. One day we were playing chase and my sister hit me. After hitting me, she ran, knocking over a large glass water jug. The huge jug with the top half broken off popped back up into a sitting position. I kept running around the tent, chasing my sister, until I caught her and returned the slap. After returning the blow, I quickly turned to run as my sister slapped my back. I fell into the broken jug in a sitting position, with the glass cutting into and across my back, blood spurting everywhere. I felt no pain, but Margrette ran down the cotton rows screaming, "Mooooooother! Annie is hurt and bleeding!"

B.T. Aplin, Billy Joe, Margrette

Mother scooped me into her arms and climbed onto a tractor Daddy was driving. She held me close while putting pressure on my back to stop the bleeding. I wasn't hurting or afraid of the blood because I was being held tight in my precious mother's loving arms. Blood did not bother my mother; when she was young, she had wanted to be a doctor. However, she could not get her education because of having to work to put her siblings through school. Education was a high priority for my mother.

The doctor immediately stitched me up as my mother kept gently caressing my arm, looking at me with her loving eyes and repeating, "You will be OK." Daddy looked on from a distance until they were finished. Then, back onto the tractor, he brought Mother and I home but returned to the fields.

People often asked, "What do you do for social fun in the country?" The answer was easy. We had peanut boils at church functions, the children played games, and at night we chased lightning bugs/fireflies. Catching the lightning bugs, we would put them into jars with holes in the lids so they could breathe, and we then watched them flicker in our rooms in the dark. A country girl's form of a nightlight!

On the farm with my sisters, we often played in the second story of the machinery and hay barn. My sister Zonie was the interior designer, having her younger siblings—Josie, Margrette, and me—moving the hay bales according to her direction. One day Zonie got the idea of tying our daddy's huge handkerchief to my furry kitten, then dropping it out of the second-story hay barn to parachute to the ground! I didn't trust my sister's bright invention. After all, my oldest brother, Doc (lovingly nicknamed Bubby), had already tried the idea of parachuting with my oldest sister, Sarah (nicknamed Noopy).

Sarah "Noopy" Aplin, B.A. "Doc" Aplin, 1939

Doc and Sarah were several years older than me, but Sarah had shared with us younger siblings how Doc convinced her to fly!

B.A. "Doc" Aplin, United States Air Force 1954

When they were young, Doc had Sarah climb up into the two-story hay barn with a tractor umbrella. The purpose was for Sarah to jump out using the umbrella as a parachute. He told her the umbrella would "float her down." So she did it! After she crashed on the ground below, and was still laying in a heap, Doc ran over and said, "No, Noopy, you did it wrong! You have to hold it like this!" Doc showed her how to angle the huge tractor umbrella. "Now, go up there and do it again!" However, Noopy had enough sense and enough aches and pains from the first fall not to listen to her older brother to "do it again!"

"No, Bubby, you do it." Doc did not want to make the jump, so their parachuting days were over. However, Doc did join the air force and became an aircraft mechanic, but he still did not want to be the one to jump!

Remembering my sister's parachuting story, I climbed out of the barn, rushing to the ground below to catch my little kitten when it failed to fly.

5

Zonie shouted down at me, "Are you ready?"

"Yes!" I replied. Margrette and Josie curiously looked on.

Whoosh out of the second-story barn door went my little kitten tied inside of my daddy's red handkerchief. I had my tiny arms stretched upward, waiting for the fall, when much to my amazement, the kitten was floating. Daddy's huge red handkerchief was the perfect parachute! Success! We were all shouting and happy like we were the original inventors of parachuting, and in our family, we were! However, when the kitten reached my protective arms, I refused to let them do it again.

Not that I wasn't creative like my older siblings; I was. I enjoyed cooking. I would take dirt and mix it with water and make biscuits like our mother. Then I placed them on the doorsteps to bake in the sun. Yes, I even tried eating my invention and serving it to my sisters. The mud biscuits tasted like dirty, uncooked grits. I thought they were good until I had to drink Daddy's concoction of turpentine to kill the worms. Yuck! No more eating dirt biscuits!

II

"KABOOM!"

Mr. and Mrs. Aplin had eight children. I will list them from the oldest to the youngest: Doc, Sarah, Rudy, Billy Joe, Zonie, Josie, Margrette, and Annie.

Billy Joe was also curious, with an inventor's heart like his seven siblings. However, the two least curious of the eight were Josie and Rudy. They were avid readers. Most of their curiosity was played out among the pages in a book.

One year on July 4, Billy Joe had been given some large firework explosions. He exploded a few and said, "Wow! If they are that loud on the ground, how much louder would they sound in Mothers huge three-legged wash pot?" With a smile on his face of great anticipation and a twinkle in his eye, he headed for the wash pot. Billy Joe yelled at us to hide behind a tree as he lit the fuse and threw it into Mother's primitive form of a washing machine. *Kaboom!* Smoke went into the air as the huge kettle blew into pieces.

With the smile completely gone from Billy Joe's face and the twinkle in his eye now reflecting shock and fear, Daddy came running only to see Mother's washing machine (of a sort) blown into pieces. In a fury, Daddy stormed off. He cut a tree limb for a switch and proceeded to give Billy Joe a serious whipping.

Daddy then drove into the city and bought Mother a brand-new ringer washing machine. No more building fires for wash pots and scrub boards for Mrs. Aplin!

For entertainment at night, we would attempt to get a show on the television, but programming in the country with an antenna was very difficult. I remember many nights watching the horizontal line roll over and over on Roy Rogers's and Dale Evan's faces on the television. Most of the time, there was static, and not any of the three channels would come into focus. We would then sit around the fireplace and sing.

We all loved singing. Daddy would play the harmonica or guitar, with him and Mother singing along. Often my sisters would tell me scary stories just to see me shove my fingers into my ears and beg them not to say anymore. Laughing, they would tell the scary story again when I removed my fingers from my ears.

We also played cards and board games. Besides, there were so many children, we made teams outside for all sorts of sports activities.

As a child, one of my favorite memories with my dad was rhyming. Daddy was an amazing poet. He would begin a poem, and I had to immediately add to it with the same theme. We would go back and forth until one of us faltered, usually me.

Daddy was not only an excellent farmer but a hunter, fisherman, athlete, and an extremely fast runner. His abilities and endurance were astonishing, as were my mother's. However, by the time the work in the fields was done, Mother's work continued: cooking dinner on the wood range, ironing with the wood-fired iron, sewing clothes for her children to wear. The work for our mother never ended. When she did have a moment to rest, she would have the Holy Bible in her hands, reading and studying it while praying for her family. The Bible is the only book I ever saw my mother read. However, she always sang along when we were singing because she could work as she sang. It wasn't until her later years that she had time to play board games or cards with all of her children.

Work was hard on the farm, but life was simple and innocent. We were a typical family of Southern farmers. We loved the Lord, loved our family, loved our country, and worked hard. With the teaching that if we received an education and continued working diligently, we could achieve anything. Even though Mother labored hard, she was the spiritual strength of our family. Daddy was the taskmaster and disciplinarian who made sure we were all completing our assigned jobs. Both strengths were at the core of our family: *faith and hard work.*

A DESTRUCTIVE TORNADO

I n 1961, when I was eight years of age, a massive tornado destroyed our cotton farm. Mother was outside bathing her youngest granddaughter, Sharon, when she heard glass crashing inside the house. Rushing inside, Mother saw me standing by a broken lamp. She then sharply scolded me for breaking the lamp. "I didn't break it," I replied in my defense. "The wind blew it over." Mother walked over to close the window and saw a huge black tornado heading straight toward our home.

She began yelling for all her children to come inside. Being a great lady of faith, Mother was trying to keep all of us children in a huddle to pray. However, Billy Joe hid under the bed. "Come out and pray with us, Billy Joe!" Mother shouted above the roar of the tornado. "I can pray just as easy under here, Mother!" Billy Joe replied.

Mother saw Margrette and I standing by a window with our faces pressed to the glass while straining to watch through the rain as the machinery and hay barn exploded. Wow, what a sight! At that point, we could feel Mother's strong hands on the back of our clothes, jerking us away from the window while scolding, "Stay away from the windows!" Mother and her now-huddled flock prayed as the sound of a train roared louder and louder overhead. Then suddenly . . . all became quiet.

Mother ordered Billy Joe and Rudy to run quickly down the country road to check on our neighbors. Doc went outside, harvesting peaches off the ground for all to eat. A little time passed, when up the road came Billy Joe and Rudy carrying the neighbors' children accompanied by the parents.

The tornado destroyed our neighbors' home, but all survived. Mother and Daddy were raised in the old prejudice South, but neither wanted to see anyone harmed. Mother was not prejudiced toward blacks at all. She was full of love and wisdom. She knew and taught that all colors were "the Good Lord's children." Mother was right.

The following day they assessed the damage. The tornado had uprooted and stripped the cotton stalks as well as the cornfields. It blew out and toppled our two-story machinery and hay barn, also uprooting huge oaks and peach trees. It laid in waste everything for more than a mile, including uprooting a giant grandfather oak that shaded our home, laying it in the opposite direction from our house. However, every other porch column was still standing, supporting our veranda. Except for the columns, our home remained untouched amid the complete ruin and devastation surrounding us. We all knew and gave credit to the Lord for His mercy and grace. We were also grateful for our mother's abiding faith and prayer.

Shortly after the tornado, I saw my daddy hammering a muddy rock. "What are you doing hitting that muddy rock, Daddy?" I asked. With a big smile on his face, Daddy replied, "This isn't a rock, baby; its an oyster!"

He then cracked it open and said "See!" and showed me the slimy-looking thing inside that reminded me of what one blew into handkerchiefs. Daddy offered one for me to eat. I tried, and it was disgusting! It was flavorless and felt cold, wet, and slimy on my tongue and gagged me when I tried to swallow it. I ran away not wanting to "try" another one. Back then, I had no idea how much I would grow to enjoy those slimy creatures.

SEAFOOD INDUSTRY

After Mother and Daddy saw their precious farm laid in waste, they decided to load up all their children and venture into a new industry in north Florida. They went from land farming to sea farming, and became commercial fishermen.

We soon discovered the seafood industry required hard work, great stamina, lots of faith, and enormous courage to be successful. Our family had it all.

Daniel "Rudy" Aplin High School Carrabelle, Florida

After three years of commercial fishing in north Florida, Daddy heard that the oysters in Texas were huge and plentiful. With their faith in the Lord, the hope of a better future, and sweat on their brow, like the great American explorers of their ancestors, they left for Texas in search of the American Dream.

The commercial seafood industry in Texas was an amazing challenge for B.T. and Sarah Aplin; however, they weathered all the difficulties. When times were rough, Daddy would hunt deer, rabbits, and squirrels for the dinner table. We always had seafood, even though as a child I did not appreciate it.

The years passed, and slowly Mother and Daddy grew their fishing ability from nothing into a modest earning. When all of their children were grown, Daddy purchased a piece of land by their home to continue with his first passion—farming.

B.T., Noopy, Sarah, Billy Joe Aplin and daughter 1968

At one time Daddy was known as the greatest peanut farmer in the state of Georgia. Yes, not more prosperous but better at peanut farming than Jimmy Carter.

Daddy also produced excellent watermelons and vegetables, and beautiful cotton crops. In Florida, before the move to Texas, Daddy grew tomatoes for sale. People drove from an hour away just to buy Mr. Aplin's delicious tomatoes. Now, in Texas, he could once again grow his crops.

In 1965 our parents purchased a small family home and in time were able to buy the adjoining land. By 1979 Mother and Daddy were happily settled into the fishing town of Seadrift, Texas, living among more than thirty of their offspring. At this time Daddy was harbormaster. He and Mother had always worked in the seafood industry as a way to make a living, but Daddy enjoyed farming. He loved bringing fresh vegetables to the table, plus sharing them with family and friends. After working hard their entire life to provide for their family, it was finally what it should have been for our parents' retirement years. Life was good.

Out of their eight children, six remained in the seafood industry. Several of their grandchildren and great-grandchildren also worked in the seafood industry. Many had boats for harvesting, fish houses for processing, plus marketing and distribution to restaurants. I lobbied in the political arena, affecting the commercial seafood industry.

The eldest, Doc Aplin, shipped blue crabs all over the USA. His creativity failed with our sister Sarah parachuting out of the two-story barn, but it succeeded with him inventing the four-eyed crab traps that increased blue crab production.

Seadrift 1977: Mr & Mrs. Aplin with only 6 of their children
and 19 of their Grandchildren.

Also, Doc accepted an invitation from China to teach the Chinese how to properly build their traps to harvest their crab industry. Later, Doc's son Brad was asked to come to China to teach the Chinese how to properly process crabmeat at their crab-picking plant. If crabmeat is not properly processed, high levels of bacteria can set in. It was during those eight months that Brad met, fell in love with, and later married his Chinese sweetheart, Ping.

In 1979 Doc had a crab business at the docks in Seadrift that bought Texas blue crabs from many crab fishermen. All of his seven children and some grandchildren also worked in the seafood industry.

B.A. "Doc" Aplin 1996

The second-oldest, Sarah—nicknamed Noopy—had an oyster house in Seadrift where one processed oysters for sale and distribution. Sarah also owned and operated an oyster boat. Several of her children were also self-employed in the commercial seafood industry.

The third-oldest child, Rudy, was in seafood as well, but more as a businessman and commercial shrimper, and he was politically involved. The fourth child was Billy Joe. He was different than his older siblings. He wasn't satisfied to run small- to medium-sized vessels. He desired to be a ship pilot. One day while having me quiz him for a college exam on navigation, I asked, "Billy Joe, why do you want to be a ship pilot?" With a snickering smile, he said, "Sis, anyone can take a ship across the ocean, but it takes someone special to bring it into port and dock it!" He knew that he was one of the few who could do it. Even though Billy Joe married when he was nineteen and had three children at a young age, he worked continuously to support them. He also went to college part-time for about ten years to get the college portion of navigation completed.

Captain Billy Joe Aplin, 1972

The fifth child is our sister Zonie. She was Daddy's favorite daughter because she was a great cook and an excellent singer. Zonie worked in the seafood industry, but her passion was singing country music. In addition, she was an excellent artist. After all, Zonie designed our family's first working parachute!

The sixth child was Josephine, nicknamed Josie. All of Mother and Daddy's children had high IQs, but some applied their intelligence more like Josie. She got married in her senior year of high school but graduated and went on to college with honors to be a biochemist. Josie was a scholar, enjoyed reading and, like her other siblings, her mathematical skills were exceptional! Josie was hired by NASA and helped map one of the NASA spaceflights to the moon. However, her brilliance did not exceed her beauty, inside and out. She was stunning! She later married a man named Dale who had served as a marine. After their marriage, he chose the crab-fishing industry.

All of my parents' children were attractive as well as intelligent and hardworking. People would often tell Mother and Daddy what beautiful daughters they had, and with a smile, Mother would say, "Pretty is as pretty does." She was determined none of her children would grow vain because of their exterior beauty. It was a love for the Lord and inner beauty of the heart that mattered to our mother. Daddy, on the other hand, enjoyed receiving compliments concerning his daughters and granddaughters.

Josephine "Josie" Aplin 9th Grade Seadrift, Texas

The seventh child, Margrette, was beautiful like Josie and her older sisters. However, where Josie excelled in scholastics, Margrette excelled in winning beauty contests. She was also a beautiful flirt! Being two years younger than Margarette, living in the shadow of her beauty, I was overjoyed when she announced she was getting married! She never liked farming or seafood. Marrying an army man at a young age, Margarette worked as a waitress to help support their family. Later she worked as a physical therapist's assistant and went to school to be an electronic engineer. Her grades in college were excellent, but unfortunately, the tragedy within this story brought an illness that changed her path in life—forever.

I, Annie, am the youngest of Mr. and Mrs. Aplin's children. My older siblings said, "You were the baby and spoiled rotten!" I would respond with a laugh and say, "I wasn't spoiled; I was just rotten!"

Mother would not let her daughters date alone; we always had to double-date or have a chaperone. When I was eleven years old, my sister Josie's boyfriend (who later became her husband) approached me while I was watching cartoons. He was going to take Josie on a date that night and asked me to refuse to go with them when Mother suggested it. I agreed, with one exception: he had to buy me a chocolate sundae. He agreed, and off to the ice cream shop we went!

Josie's Boyfriend, Josie 16-yrs old.

That evening as he and Josie were leaving for the movies, Mother said, "Annie Laura, I want you to go with them." "Okay," I replied, knowing I had just gotten an ice cream sundae out of Josie's boyfriend but now a movie! If looks could kill, I would have been dead, but he knew he could not say a word. Yes, I was rotten.

I also married at a young age. Like Margrette, I did not enjoy the seafood industry because the work was smelly and dirty. I did not mind it being hard work, but I didn't like it being dirty. Little did we know that the oyster mud splattering our faces as we worked was helping keep our skin soft, clear, and beautiful. It wasn't fashionable yet, but we had our own free mud treatments!

Even though I married a man who was not in the seafood industry, a year after our marriage he chose to become a commercial shrimper. We bought our first steel-hull shrimp boat named the *Annie Laura*.

When I was twenty-four I became an effective Texas state lobbyist, lobbying on behalf of the commercial seafood industry. Amazing how at eleven years of age my maneuvering with my future brother-in-law paid off in the political arena. Years later I became an officer for the Hays County Sheriff's Department, then a Christian missionary serving in many countries, such as Cuba, China, Venezuela, Haiti, Jamaica, and several other countries, but my main call of service was in Cuba. Ironically, I was named after a missionary, Sister Annie Laura Toller, of Blakely, Georgia.

Annie, Ronnie, and Ronnie Jr.

In 1979 my husband and I lived in Plano, Texas, with our two small children. We owned a flourishing fresh seafood market that I managed in Richardson, Texas. On weekdays I took the children to school, then picked them up and brought them to the market while I worked. Most nights I had to work late, processing the seafood after my employees went home. However, both of my children enjoyed working and would clock in and help me around the business until closing. Occasionally they would clock out and watch cartoons in my cozy homelike office. My husband operated and lived aboard a large steel-hull shrimp boat on the coast of Texas. I was involved with the chamber of commerce as well as lobbied for the seafood industry in Austin, Texas, when the state legislature was in session. Life was extremely busy but productive and good.

For eighteen years my parents and family had worked hard in the face of many obstacles, such as severe weather and numerous government regulations of the seafood industry. It was physically demanding but a good life. One born out of many years of struggle but finally a place of comfort and retirement for my parents, B.T. and Sarah Aplin. Also a wonderful place for their children and grandchildren to live.

In addition to strict government regulations, there were also the unwritten laws of work and respect for fellow fishermen on the water. Those laws no one can regulate. It has to come from one's heart, with honesty and integrity. In this revealing true story, both laws will be played out in very heart-wrenching discoveries.

FAILED ATTEMPT ON THE LIFE OF BILLY JOE AND FAMILY

L et's start with my youngest brother, Billy Joe Aplin, and his family.

Captain Billy Joe Aplin

In 1979 Billy Joe was ready to begin his new career as a Houston ship pilot. Circumstances caused the pilot position to be delayed. Billy Joe then bought a crab-fishing boat and traps. He knew seafood was something he could do to support his family until things opened up as a ship pilot. Billy Joe packed up his wife and three children and moved them to Seadrift, Texas.

Shortly after Billy Joe and his family were settled in, he noticed his oldest brother, Doc, wasn't buying blue crabs from the Vietnamese fisherman. He asked, "Why?"

"Because they are different than us, Billy Joe," Doc replied. He continued "They don't think like we do. They don't act like we do. They have created a lot of problems for the people here, including your family, Billy Joe. You don't understand because you haven't lived here and had to deal with all the issues."

"Of course I know y'all have had issues. Mother and Daddy have told me about their concerns. Doc, some are just trying to make a living for their family just like we are. Why don't you buy from a few Vietnamese and see how that goes?" Billy Joe replied.

Frustrated, Doc said, "You don't understand. Many have stolen from other fishermen! They have purchased boats with government loans that have interest so cheap. *We* could never get a loan so low. Plus they get government aid in several other ways. It helps them undercut our prices and is driving many Americans out of business. Several have intimidated Americans with their scare tactics—cutting crab buoys, running other fishermen's crab traps and stealing them blind! They have even tried running over American children with their cars! They even sank Noopy's boat! Your nephew, Jerry, had to start carrying a gun on the water because of their intimidating threats. For two years Daddy has tried to get the government involved to get the Vietnamese assimilation training or some type of training. He was hoping they would quit acting like they are still at war and we are the enemy. Daddy told the *Fisherman's News* magazine that he is afraid someone is going to die if the government doesn't step in and do something. No, you haven't lived here for far too many years, Billy Joe. You really do not know these people, and you don't understand."

"OK. I know it's been bad, Doc, but I have met these three crab fishermen that seem to be nice and just want to work and take care of their families. How about buying from them?" Billy Joe pleaded.

Running his fingers through his hair with a stressful look of impending dangers, Doc agreed, "OK, Billy Joe, I will buy from these three and no others, and let's see how that goes. Tell them I will buy their crabs."

Smiling, Billy Joe said, "Thanks, Bubby!" Doc's childhood nickname always made him smile.

Billy Joe quickly found the fishermen and proudly announced they could sell their produce to his brother. With great joy the three Vietnamese boats began bringing their harvest into Doc's dock. My niece and nephew, Regina and Jerry Jeter, gladly taught one of the crab fishermen, Duke Tran, how to crab. Duke was very grateful for their kindness. All was going well.

Billy Joe began running his crab traps with his wife and three children on board. They all loved the water, and even though this was work, it was excellent family time on the bay.

Each day the children were not in school, they would rise early with their parents, watching the beautiful morning sun come up. Then they would go with their mom and dad, watching their dad loading the fresh crab bait on board the boat.

Afterward, with the red-and-gold morning sun reflecting on the smooth water, they set off to run their crab traps and see what harvest they would find. The cool breeze blew through their hair when their dad opened the boat's motor wide-open, gliding at high speeds on the top of the glassy water. It was such a free feeling speeding along the bay approaching the crab lines, excited over what each day would bring! Every day in a fisherman's life is one of hope in a productive and prosperous day.

Crab fishing is similar to lobster fishing in the sense that it's traps with fish bait inside to lure the lobster or crab into the trap. These wire mesh crab traps—or pots—have what is called a bait well in the center of the trap. These bait wells hold the dead fish bait that lures the blue crabs in through the four openings, called eyes. The wire trap is in the shape of a box with one eye-opening on each side of the trap. The reason the crab pot is called a trap is because crabs can crawl in, but they can't crawl out (if the eye is properly set). With a four-eyed crab trap, crabs can enter from any direction.

There is a rope attached to the trap on one end and a buoy to float the trap on top of the water on the other end. The buoy has a marker with information attached to prove who owns the trap.

When the crab boat approaches the trap line (called the line because the buoys are separated by several feet and are arranged when possible in a straight line on the water), the fisherman uses a gaff hook (a long pole with a metal hook on the end) to reach over the boat to grab under the buoy and pull the crab pot on board. One side of the pot is open, with a hook strapping it shut. Once it's on board, the fishermen pick the pot up, unhook the open side of the pot, and shake the crabs out into a wooden crate. They must be very careful not to get bitten by the crabs' fierce snapping claws! Once they harvest the crabs and put fresh bait into all of their crab pot bait wells, they head back to shore to sell their produce while the crabs are still alive. Crabs have no monetary value if they are dead; therefore, speed in crab harvest production and distribution is important.

Life was going excellently for Billy Joe and his family. For years Billy Joe was well-known in newspapers and other media sources for his excelling ability to locate the best red snapper fishing holes. Now he was discovering the best blue crab locations. He bought his family a home in an upscale neighborhood and continued going forward in the blue crab fishing industry. However, Billy Joe never gave up on his desire to work as a ship pilot.

In the summer of 1979, the day was no different from the next. It was sunny and warm, with calm seas. School was out, so Billy Joe brought his wife and three children to work with him. As they were running their crab trap line, he spotted another boat running his line. They appeared to be stealing from my brother and his

28

family! As Billy Joe approached, he saw it was a Vietnamese crab boat and that the Vietnamese fisherman had his traps intermingled with Billy Joe's.

There is an unwritten law on the water with a *code of honor* among fishermen that you never drop your crab trap between another crab fisherman's lines. Two reasons: First, it cuts down on the production of the fisherman who first dropped his traps in the area. Second, it discourages stealing. If one's traps are intermingled and you spot a crab fisherman running his traps, he could be running yours as well! Therefore, intermingling traps was a huge no-no!

When the Vietnamese man saw Billy Joe and his family approaching, he stopped running traps. He stopped his boat and sat with his arms folded, glaring over at Billy Joe. He knew he had been caught, but the Vietnamese man continued his intimidating stare, arms folded with a look of "Nothing you can do to me. I will do as I want."

Billy Joe picked up one of the Vietnamese man's traps and shouted, "You are mixed in my line! You have to move your pots." No response from the Vietnamese man. Billy Joe thought maybe he didn't speak English, so he shouted "Move your pots over here and out of my line!"—motioning where he was to move the traps. No response; just the same intimidating glare.

Billy Joe then took his pot to the area where he could move them to and dropped it, pointing, saying, "Move your traps over here and get them out of my line!" Still no response from the Vietnamese man—only the same fixed, intimidating stare.

Billy Joe then went back to his line, gaff-hooked and picked up another of the Vietnamese man's crab traps, and again shouted, "Move your traps over here!" Again no response, just glares.

Billy Joe then took his trap and stomped on it, motioning as he said, "If you don't move your traps out of my line, I'm going to crush them!" That got a response.

The Vietnamese man took off in his boat, leaving his traps behind. Billy Joe thought, "Oh, my. He is up to no good and is going to come back and cut my buoys" He, his wife, and their three children returned to running their crab trap line.

Suddenly, from behind the small islands dotting the bay, came six Vietnamese boats at full speed surrounding and ramming Billy Joe and his family's boat. Billy Joe was an excellent boatman, but they had his boat surrounded and trapped.

The Vietnamese fishermen continued ramming his boat, with the children crying and screaming in hysteria. Billy Joe kept the throttle forward, trying to find or push a break between the boats. One of the Vietnamese men jumped into the water with a huge knife between his teeth, trying to grab hold of Billy Joe's boat and climb on board. Billy Joe shouted at his wife, "Take the wheel and keep pushing forward. I will jump into the water; then maybe they will let you and the children go!"

"No!" screamed his wife and children, begging him to stay.

Then suddenly he was able to break their boat free!

Pressing the throttle at full speed, he headed to shore. However, the six boats—three in front and three behind—escorted him in a threatening manner all the way to the dock. Upon arrival, the Vietnamese boats turned back onto the bay.

Billy Joe and his family's narrow escape from death had them deeply shaken. They called the police and game wardens to come to the docks and take a report.

Oddly enough, the police said there was nothing they could do because they were on the water. All of the authorities went on to say, "They are aliens, not citizens; therefore, they fall under different laws. The most we can do is give the Vietnamese man with the knife trying to climb into your boat a twenty-five-dollar fine for the weapon." Much was not heard by my brother after the twenty-five-dollar-fine statement for attempted murder.

Billy Joe knew maritime law—he had studied it for years—so he quoted the statutes of what would happen to him if he committed those crimes. "Yes, that's you, Billy Joe. You are an American citizen, but different laws apply to aliens."

In fury at his family almost being murdered on the water that day, Billy Joe went home, picked up his one-hundred-ton captain's license, drove back to the bay, tore it up, and threw it into the water, saying, "These are not worth anything!" He then drove his very shaken and fearful family home.

My brother was very much a family man and took them with him everywhere. He knew with this kind of lawlessness, for the protection of his loved ones, he could not stay in the crab fishing industry. He sold his lucrative crab business to our cousin, Donald Ray, then began working on rigging his boat for commercial shrimping. The Vietnamese had not pushed to take over the shrimping industry—yet.

Billy Joe Aplin, Seadrift, Texas 1979

Shortly after the event on the water, the Vietnamese crabbers who sold their crabs to our brother Doc approached Billy Joe with a piece of paper. As the Vietnamese men shoved the paper into Billy Joe's hand, they shouted a warning: "They Kill You! They Kill You!"

Billy Joe opened the paper they had given him, observing six names listed. He went home and gave the paper to his wife to put away for evidence. Billy Joe then called an insurance company and took out a huge life insurance policy. My brother wanted to be sure if the worse happened, his family would be taken care of. He finally understood what Doc had been trying to tell him, but he knew all Vietnamese people were by no means bad.

VI

MURDER OF BILLY JOE APLIN

On July 22, 1979 Billy Joe's thirty-fifth birthday was beautiful, with the usual celebration. His children bought him a new golf shirt and a cake with candles, and sang songs of many more happy birthdays. It was a beautiful and blessed summer day.

On August 2, 1979, Billy Joe continued working on his boat, readying it for shrimping. He had been welding his new shrimping rig, and the welding burned his eyes. Billy Joe went home and tried caring for them himself, but the burn in one eye was too intense.

The following day, August 3, 1979, he put on his beautiful birthday shirt his children had given him and drove to the nearest hospital in Port Lavaca. The doctors treated both of his eyes. They bandaged the one with the severe burn and sent Billy Joe home. Usually Billy Joe's family went everywhere with him, but that day no one wanted to sit around a hospital for hours; therefore, Billy Joe was traveling alone.

When he arrived back in Seadrift and was driving past the docks, he spotted the six Vietnamese men who had tried killing him and his family. Billy Joe quickly pulled off the main road and parked by the waterfront highway. With his eyes hurting from the burn and one eye bandaged, he walked over to the six men and began shouting at them while pointing toward the bay. "If you ever try killing my family again, you better watch out when you are on the water!"

All six men shouted back at Billy Joe in Vietnamese, jumped into their car, and took off. However, as Billy Joe started to get back into his truck and leave, an elderly Vietnamese man kept him at the wharf, talking with him. The reason soon became clear.

As suddenly as out on the water, the car full of the Vietnamese men reappeared, speeding down to where the elderly Vietnamese man had delayed Billy Joe from leaving. One jumped out with a handgun, securing it with a military hold and stance, aimed at Billy Joe. Another had a rifle.

Billy Joe threw his arms into the air in a sign of surrender, yelling, "No, man, not that! Not that!" Arms high in the air, he turned to run as the Vietnamese man with the handgun fired the first bullet straight through his heart, severing Billy Joe's aorta. As the bullet ripped through his flesh, Billy Joe fell.

Even though blood was pumping into my brother's body with every beat of his heart, he was able to get off the ground and scramble for cover behind his small pickup truck. The Vietnamese men chasing him, guns in hand, began closing in on Billy Joe from behind his truck, where he was hiding. Billy Joe then ran toward the onlookers standing by the highway as the Vietnamese men continued shooting at him from the back.

Several witnesses were watching at the waterfront that day. They testified that the Vietnamese man with the handgun, after shooting my brother, started running at Billy Joe, continuing to shoot. The witnesses said, "The Vietnamese man appeared to be aiming at Billy Joe's head."

When Billy Joe reached the people who were watching in shock and fear on the side of the road, he crumpled and fell at their feet. Looking up at them, clutching his chest, Billy Joe cried out, "My God, help me! Help me!"

One of the onlookers was our ten-year-old nephew, who had heard the shots and came running to see what he thought was fireworks . . . only to see his uncle writhing in agonizing pain, lying in a bloody heap.

When Billy Joe fell, the Vietnamese men ran back to their car and sped away.

Onlookers said, "It seemed forever before the ambulance arrived." It was later reported that Billy Joe passed away on his way to the hospital. He bled out. Others said he died at the hospital.

News and media outlets were quick to swoop in and swarm upon the events. However, their reporting was sloppy (or intentional) and did not follow the actual events at all.

One news source reported: "Three boats burned and a house firebombed, which led to the killing of a white man." How wrong. Meanwhile, our parents, who had pleaded for help from the government for at least two years, expressing grave concerns that someone would die if the government did not intervene with the Vietnamese. Now, one of our own lay dead in a cold morgue.

VII

"FIVE MORE TO DIE!"

That same dreadful day—August 3, 1979—Mother and Daddy were vacationing with my family and me at a dear friend's ranch near Bandera, Texas, in the hill country. My husband and I wanted some relaxed family time before school and shrimp season started. This was the perfect location! After all, it was where we had spent our honeymoon.

Annie's children: Ronnie Jr. & Angel playing in pool overflow
Bandera, TX August 3, 1979

It was a lovely summer day in the hill country. The ranch had a beautifully artisan-crafted, spring-fed swimming pool on the bank of the river. The river ran beside an old renovated Native American hut. Mother and Daddy, both having Native American roots, found the cabin and the entire area fascinating. The river was rich in abundance of fish and the ranch full of wildlife. Also, the soil was perfect for farming, with its own natural springwater. What an excellent location for the Native Americans who first lived there.

Mother looked at me and said, "Call Doc and give him this phone number in case of an emergency."

I contested with, "Mother, there won't be an emergency." Mother insisted, "Call your brother and give him this number."

I was an obedient daughter, and she seemed determined, so I made the call. In 1979 one did not have mobile phones like they do today; you made calls from a hardwired landline.

That day after exploring the hills, hiking the river, and swimming in the pool, we all settled down for dinner. Our family friend was an excellent hostess, serving delicious Texas barbecue with all the trimmings.

After joyful fellowship over dinner, with the dishes cleaned and put away, bedtime was drawing near. My husband walked over to the television to turn on the 10:00 p.m. news when the phone rang. Our hostess said, "Answer it."

Ronnie answered the phone. Looking at the floor as he faced the wall, obviously shaken, raking his hands through his hair, he said, "Yes. Yes. OK. OK."

As he hung up the phone, he turned to look at us while still raking his hands through his hair. Ronnie's face was pale from the call. He stood staring at us, speechless.

"What's wrong?" Mother pleaded. Ronnie did not answer. "Tell us what's wrong," she again begged, with a look of dread upon her face.

Holding back his own horror and tears, "Billy Joe has been shot," Ronnie let out with a gasp.

Mother, clutching her heart, began running in circles around the dinning table asking, "Is he dead? Is he dead?" Then diarrhea began flowing down her legs from the trauma of it all.

"I don't know," Ronnie replied with a sigh. But I knew my husband, and he did not look like he was telling the truth.

I looked up at Ronnie from the couch where I was sitting facing the dining room, and I mouthed without a sound, "Is he dead?" Ronnie nodded his head "yes," confirming mine and my parents' greatest fear. I was so gripped by grief that I ran outside and began crying and vomiting. We did not have the details yet, and at that point my parents did not know Billy Joe was dead.

I have always been thankful that my brother Doc called before my husband turned on the evening news. I was also grateful that Mother insisted I give Doc the phone number to my friend's ranch. Through silence and tears, we loaded our vehicles with children, suitcases, and vacation toys. We bid our precious hostess good-bye and set out on what seemed like a long journey back to Seadrift. However, before we left, in private my friend and our hostess asked me if my brother was dead.

I told her, "Yes."

She said, "I feel horrible for your mother. When my daughter died in a car wreck, the grief almost killed me! Take care of your mom."

"I will," I replied as I hugged her neck and kissed her good-bye. Ironically, as we were driving back to Seadrift, with Mother and Daddy's vehicle in front of ours, they had a flat tire. As Ronnie was helping Daddy change the tire, I thought, "Isn't it odd, in all of this grief and tragedy, things in life go on as though nothing has happened?" Somehow with my Christian faith, this flat tire brought a sense of normalcy into my life at the moment when I needed it most. At that time, I did not know how much I would have to remain in prayer, calmly balanced and focused, for the days, weeks, and years to come.

In Seadrift our family was gathered at Mother and Daddy's home waiting for our arrival. When my parents walked in, my siblings shared the tragic news with Mother and Daddy that their youngest son, Billy Joe, was dead. Tears again flowed, with the children trying to remain strong for our parents.

As Daddy drew a breath and strength to speak through his tears, he asked, "Who did it?"

One of the children recounted the day's events to our parents. Then Daddy asked, "Are his murderers in jail?" "No. They fled," Noopy replied.

"They fled? Are the police hunting them?" Daddy asked.

"Yes. News reported that when they fled, the police formed a manhunt to find them," one of the children replied.

Shortly after our arrival, dawn came up with its usual bright and welcoming beauty. With little rest for any of our family, several of us ventured out to speak with the locals about the previous day's events. None of us could have been prepared for what happened next. There were news reporters everywhere! They were speaking to anyone who moved and was willing to open his or her mouth.

It did not seem to matter whether their source was knowledgeable of the events or not.

One news source approached me for my opinion just as they had my siblings. With grief tightening my throat, I said, "For at least two years, my daddy has been pleading with the government to step in and do something about the lawlessness of the Vietnamese crabbers. Now my brother is lying cold in the morgue, dead. My concern is how many more are going to die?" As I pointed toward the edge of Seadrift, I continued, "Look at what the government is doing. They have placed protection around the Vietnamese village when we are the ones dying!" Enough said, I then walked away.

I bought a morning newspaper and read the words "Three boats burned and a house firebombed, which led to the killing of a white man." How twisted, and a lie! However, that lie soon echoed on newsreels around the world, darkening and smearing the truth. I knew from that twisted article that I could not trust the news. Therefore, I would not permit them to interview me, and I tried to get my siblings not to speak with reporters. The reports only twisted my family's words and actions, putting them in the most destructive light. I was a state lobbyist for the commercial seafood industry and was not going to allow the news to twist my words and smear my good name. However, I could not stop my family's good name from being smeared worldwide through the twisted lies of the media.

As the day dragged on and the reality of the prior day's events began settling in the minds of the locals, my brother Rudy and I stood in the middle of the highway speaking with people to calm them down. Lines of cars were stopping full of fear and rage at what they knew had been cold-blooded murder.

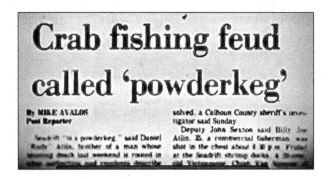

Crab fishing feud called 'powderkeg'

By MIKE AVALOS
Post Reporter

Seadrift "is a powderkeg," said Daniel Ratli... Atlis, brother of a man whose ... much had weekend is routed in...

solved, a Calhoun County sheriff's inves-
tigator said Sunday

Deputy John Sexton said Billy Joe Atlin, 25, a commercial fisherman, was shot in the chest about 4:30 p.m. Friday at the Seadrift shrimp docks. A ... old Vietnamese, Chanh Van...

Many of the American citizens had loaded guns, telling Rudy and me that they were ready to march on the Vietnamese village and fight! We pleaded with them not too. We begged, "Please, let the law take care of it! They will find the murderers and they will be convicted for their crimes. The news is twisting everything you do and say to make it look like the Vietnamese killers are the victims. *Please don't do anything.* Let the authorities handle it."

Rudy and I also asked numerous locals what really happened with the three burned boats and a firebombed house.

"Is that true?" we asked. "Yes," was the reply.

"What happened?" asked Rudy.

One man spoke up. "After the word was out from the witnesses of how Billy Joe was gunned down by the Vietnamese fishermen, the anger and frustration from all we have suffered at the Vietnamese's hands, and now the cold-blooded murder of Billy Joe, war has broken out! Someone firebombed one of the Vietnamese fishermen's homes. However, the Vietnamese men themselves burned the three Vietnamese boats because they sell crabs to Doc, and they were Billy Joe's friends. Also, they had warned Billy Joe he was going to be murdered." The Vietnamese men not only burned Duke Tran's boat and the other two boats, but they also burned Duke's home in Houston.

Seeing hunting rifles inside the car, Rudy shouted, "But we can't retaliate like this! We must let the authorities take care of it and justice be done!"

I was standing by my brother's side in agreement as he pleaded with everyone not to take action, to let the government do it. At that time we trusted our government and believed there was true justice in our judicial system. We also thought there were laws to protect us from the news printing lies. At that time we believed these things. At that time . . .

As evening drew near, my sister Noopy and I drove through town to locate the house that had been firebombed by a Molotov cocktail. A Molotov cocktail is a bottle filled with gas, or any flammable explosive fluid, with a rag tucked inside with a portion hanging out as a wick to start it burning. We were informed that the person threw the bottle of explosive against a Vietnamese person's home in retaliation for the murder of Billy Joe Aplin. No, it was not an Aplin, and to this date we do not know who truly did it; however, we have our assumptions.

The bottle exploding against the home scorched the side of the house. News cameras were in the front yard interviewing whoever would come to speak with them. As Noopy's vehicle turned the corner on the road so we could see if the home had suffered damage in the back of the house, the sight we saw amazed us!

A Vietnamese family was in the backyard of what appeared to be their scorched home. The man looked to be coaching the woman and children to go and speak with the news. Out back they appeared happy and laughing, but as the man remained behind the house and sent the woman and children out front, they pulled on their clothes to make themselves look tattered. Their shoulders slumped and their smiles turned into sad faces, with their heads hanging down. Behind the house a happy family with a neat appearance, but out front, only the woman and children looking downtrodden and sad. They portrayed the poor, scared refugee part perfectly. What a spectacle for the evening news!

Noopy and I were not surprised, but we were truly amazed at catching them doing this performance. If only the news would have done their due diligence.

My oldest sister and I continued to the waterfront where our brother was gunned down. It was difficult to go there, but we gathered every ounce of courage and leaned on our faith in the Lord and each other as support.

As Noopy pulled her vehicle down to the waterfront, parking by our brother's truck, we held each other and began to weep. Oh, how difficult it was to see where he had died, but what we saw next only intensified our pain.

As we got out of the vehicle in horror, we began looking around. There on the ground and on the side of Billy Joe's truck was his blood. A lot of blood. Tears were flowing nonstop for the loss of our brother, but seeing this bloody mess only made the reality of his murder and the pain he suffered even more acute.

Tears, grief, and fear did not stop us from our investigation of the events. Noopy began going over and pointing out to me every piece of the exterior of our brother's truck. She pointed to the puddle of blood by his truck then the blood smears on the side where he had first been shot. Noopy then pointed to other blood smears with Billy Joe's handprints going all the way behind his truck to the other side. This supported what we had heard about the first shot taking him to the ground but that he got up and was scrambling around his truck to get away from the continuing gunshots coming his way. The enormous strength that it took for my baby brother to have gotten up and tried so hard to get away from his ensuing murderers, while blood was pouring into and out of his body, still astounds me.

Noopy and I had heard about the events surrounding Billy Joe's murder, but we needed to hear exactly what happened from the eyewitnesses. With more factual knowledge but even heavier hearts than when we had arrived at the waterfront, we began driving to the homes of some of the witnesses.

As Noopy and I arrived at the home of the first witness, a sixteen-year-old teenager, his parents greeted us with hugs and invited us into their home. My sister, struggling to hold back her tears, asked, "Is your son here? We need to know what happened."

"No, he is not here," the young man's parents replied. "When can I speak with him?" Noopy asked.

In apparent distress, with a look of fear, clenching her fingers then wringing her hands, the young man's mother replied, "I'm so sorry, Noopy, but we sent him and his two friends out of town to keep them in hiding. We are afraid the Vietnamese will kill them too because they are witnesses to Billy Joe's murder!"

Both Noopy and I agreed that it was safest for the young men to be hidden, but we couldn't help but wonder, with this much fear, if the parents would allow their children to testify.

Noopy asked the parents to repeat their son's testimony about Billy Joe being shot. Noopy said, "We heard some of the events, but we need to know exactly what happened to our brother."

The young man's parents began recounting the events that had been conveyed to them:

"Billy Joe walked over to the men and began shouting at them that if they ever tried killing his family again, they better watch out on the water! All six men, shouting back in Vietnamese, jumped into their car and sped off. As Billy Joe started to get into his truck to leave, an elderly Vietnamese man kept him at the wharf talking with him. Billy Joe got out of his truck and began speaking with the old Vietnamese man.

"It seemed as suddenly as the car had left, it again arrived with the six Vietnamese men. They sped down to the water, where the elderly Vietnamese man and Billy Joe were standing. The first man jumped out with a handgun. Another had a rifle. The first man secured the gun with both hands in what appeared to be a military hold and stance and aimed the gun directly at Billy Joe. Billy Joe threw his arms into the air in a sign of surrender, yelling, 'No, man, not that! Not that!' Arms high in the air, Billy Joe turned to run.

"The Vietnamese man with the handgun began firing. The first bullet hit Billy Joe. After Billy Joe was hit, his body slammed to the ground. He then pulled himself up off the ground and scrambled behind his pickup truck. The Vietnamese men were chasing after him, bullets flying. They began closing in on Billy Joe from behind his truck, so Billy Joe then ran toward our son and the others by the highway. Our son said as Billy Joe ran up the embankment toward them, the Vietnamese men continued shooting at him from the back but were obviously aiming toward his head. Our son also said there were several others who witnessed what happened, including your nephew Phillip. He too was standing on the side of the road.

"As Billy Joe reached the top of the embankment, he fell at our son's feet clutching his chest and cried out, 'My God, help me! Help me!' They were all horrified at what was happening and terrified at what might happen to them, but no one could move; they were all frozen with fear. When the Vietnamese men saw Billy Joe on the ground writhing in agonizing pain, lying in a pool of blood, they ran to their car and sped away. Our son said it seemed to take the ambulance forever to get to him." This was the report of the incident that had already been conveyed to us but was now verified by the teenager's mother.

Noopy asked, "Did you know that the first shot severed Billy Joe's aorta?" The young man's family sat in pained silence at that knowledge, as well as obvious concern and fear for their child.

"No, we didn't know," they sadly responded.

Noopy continued, "The bullet went in one side and out the other straight through his heart, severing Billy Joe's aorta. If he had not held his arms up to surrender, the bullet wouldn't have killed him. The pain our brother suffered lying on the ground with blood pouring into his abdomen . . . I can't imagine how he must have been suffering." Noopy then began weeping. I placed my arm around my precious sister to comfort and calm her.

With the darkness of night coming on, we thanked the young man's parents and headed back toward our parent's home.

That night was also long with grief over Billy Joe's death, filled with concern that his murderers were running free somewhere to kill again.

As morning drew near, the day was filled with more frustration and anger. It appeared that everywhere you went there was a media camera and/or newspaperman—as well as police and government agents—but Billy Joe's murderers had not yet been found.

The U.S. Justice Department, Mr. Bob Alexander, was trying to keep a lid on the civil war that had broken out after Billy Joe's murder. News article (Sunday, August 12, 1979, Seadrift, Texas (AP)...Peter Van Tho, the US Catholic Conference refugee representative who arrived here Friday with Justice Department mediator Robert Alexander. The two plan to remain throughout the weekend. The problem, said Alexander, isn't merely local squabble. There are some trends here we are concerned with," he said. "Bad publicity at a time close on the heels of President Carter's increasing Vietnamese immigration allocation does not do that any good"...

Our family was struggling to wrap our heads around the death of our brother, my parent's son—a husband, father, uncle, and friend. While the news only wanted headlines. What surprised us was that the police were protecting the Vietnamese fishermen, while Americans were the ones always threatened and now dying. It didn't make sense. Nothing made sense.

Television and newspaper reporters were vicious, portraying big, bad Americans trying to keep poor, little struggling Vietnamese people from working. The twisted truths and total lies compounded my family's grief and fear of more reprisal. To add to our pain, news commentators were everywhere, shoving cameras into our faces. Every time one of us would surface from our home, the news looked like vultures ascending upon their prey. I understand it is the media's job to get the story, but they should be concerned about getting the story accurately, *not* just getting a story.

My parents' phone rang. Mother picked it up. "Hello? Hello?" Momentary silence on the other end, so she hung up.

The phone rang again. Mother picked it up again. "Hello?"

A voice rang out loudly, "Five more to die! Five more to die!"

They hung up suddenly, leaving Mother trembling at the horror of more of her family being murdered. Her son's murderers were still running free. The phone call was reported, but the actions of the authorities were even more confusing.

Strangely, extra police protection was placed at the entrance to what had become known as Vietnam Village in Seadrift—to protect the Vietnamese residents, not us. *No one* was stationed outside of my parents' home or any of my family's homes. We were the ones being threatened and now murdered. This too was an event that stunned not only my family but every American in Seadrift. Now no Americans were safe. None of us could wrap our minds around the events that had unfolded and were unfolding. Police protection was provided only for the Vietnamese. This was America, not Vietnam!

We thought we had laws to protect the American citizens and the innocent. We also thought we had laws to protect us against media saying and printing lies, but they continued to do it. I wondered, shouldn't there be police posted at my parents' home and the homes of everyone who was still being threatened? Trust of my country and its laws to protect its citizens faded with every threat and false or twisted news report. However, my family still held out hope that when Billy Joe's murderers were found, there would be justice in our court of law.

Our cousin Donald Ray was the family member who had bought Billy Joe's crab fishing business. He lived a two-hour drive from Seadrift. The day following Billy Joe's murder, Donald Ray was rushing to Seadrift to be with his grieving family. Suddenly, in the dark, sirens started. Donald Ray was pulled over by the Rock Port Police and taken to jail for speeding. He called my mother, asking her to send someone to Port Lavaca to pay his bail for speeding and get him out of jail.

Mother first asked me to go. I responded, "No, Mother, I can't. I had a horrible nightmare last night and dreamed I was on a back road at night being chased by Vietnamese people in cars. There was a deep, muddy ditch on each side of the two-lane road. Maybe we can pay his fine here in Seadrift and not have to drive to Port Lavaca tonight?" Mother agreed.

I asked my sister Zonie to drive me to the Seadrift Sheriff's Department to pay Donald Ray's speeding fine and get him out of jail. Zonie first said, "I don't want to. Quit being silly about a dream and go by yourself."

"My dream is not silly, Zonie. I truly believe it is a warning from the Lord."

Zonie knew that I was not the type to fear, but she continued to try and get me to go alone. After stubborn resistance on my part from what Zonie thought was a ridiculous dream, Zonie reluctantly agreed to drive.

As we were getting into her sporting pickup, her daughter Lana shouted, "Mom, I want to come!"

"Get in!" Zonie replied. The three of us had no idea the danger that would soon be played out from my dream.

The three of us pulled up to the sheriff's department, went in, and began sharing with the small-town sheriff about our cousin's arrest in Port Lavaca.

Zonie asked, "Can we pay Donald Ray's speeding fine here so we do not have to drive to Port Lavaca tonight?"

Port Lavaca was about a thirty-minute drive up a country road. There was only one way in and one way out from Seadrift. There was nothing but woods in between the two towns, and it was late at night.

The sheriff looked pleasant and willing but said, "I have to call the Port Lavaca Sheriff's Department to get it OK'd."

The sheriff sat behind his desk with the three of us sitting on the other side facing him as he made the call. We were all hopeful. The sheriff dialed a number and conveyed the information.

Suddenly silence. The color drained from his face as he began Running his fingers across his forehead with his free hand. "Ok. Ok," He kept saying. It was obvious that the Seadrift sheriff was distressed by whatever he was hearing on the other end of the phone. This greatly concerned us.

As the call ended, the sheriff attempted to hang up the phone but was nervous and trembling so badly he could not place the phone in its cradle. He then took both of his hands to hang the phone up properly.

With color still drained from his face and trying to avoid eye contact with us, he gave instructions on what we must do. "Zonie," he said, "you have to drive to Port Lavaca. When you arrive, go to the twenty-four-hour store near the jail, use the pay phone, and call this number. This will let the jail authorities know that you are there so that when you arrive at the jail, they will unlock the doors and let you in." With a true look of concern in his eyes, he then looked at us and added, "I'm sorry." We did not understand why, but we followed the sheriff's instructions.

The three of us walked out of the sheriff's office, loaded ourselves back into Zonie's truck, and headed down the long, dark road toward Port Lavaca. We were disappointed that the fine could not be paid in Seadrift, but we were more puzzled by how nervous the sheriff had appeared. Between the three of us, there was no understanding of what we had just witnessed.

It was about 2:00 a.m. as we arrived in Port Lavaca at our instructed destination. Zonie exited the vehicle, leaving her daughter, Lana, and I sitting inside. Using the pay phone at the twenty-four-hour store, per instructions, Zonie called the phone number given to her by the sheriff. She spoke with whom she believed to be someone at the county jail and informed him that she had arrived to pay Donald Ray's fine. The man on the phone said, "Come on over to the jail, and we will unlock the doors for you."

While Zonie was on the pay phone at the twenty-four-hour store speaking with what she believed to be the county jail, my attention was drawn to a car in the parking lot of the store. A man was sitting behind his steering wheel obviously staring at Lana and I, then looking over toward the phone booth at Zonie. He had dress suits hanging in the back seat of his car. Lana and I also noticed a lot of cars on the road for that time in the morning. Normally at 2:00 a.m. the roads are empty. Everyone would be home.

After Zonie climbed back into the vehicle, I began pointing out the man in the parking lot with the dress clothes hanging in his car. However, as I pointed him out, the car took off.

Zonie said, "He was probably passing through."

I responded, "I felt he was watching us."

Lana and I also pointed out the abundance of traffic on the highway. Zonie, ignoring our concerns, said, "You are acting paranoid. The bar probably just closed."

I pondered my sister's words and said, "Paranoid? After all that's happened? Maybe."

As per Zonie's instructions on the pay telephone, she drove to the jail and parked exactly where she was informed. Leaving Lana and I in the vehicle, she went inside to pay the fine.

While Zonie was in the jail, Lana and I noticed cars going back and forth on the neighboring side roads by the jail and again shared, "How odd."

Zonie paid the fine and returned to her truck. As she cranked up her vehicle, once again we pointed out all of the cars racing back and forth down the roads on each side of the jail. Now even Zonie was surprised. This was a very out-of-the-way location and not an active thoroughfare. Zonie drove away from the jail, heading back through Port Lavaca toward Seadrift.

Zonie put her left turn blinker on as we slowed for the last traffic light in town. Once we turned at this light, we would be going down a dark country road back to Seadrift.

As we approached the green light, cars suddenly sped up, coming out of nowhere. One moved in front of us as Zonie's truck turned left onto the country road, and one car closed in behind.

To our shock, Lana and I got a good look at the advancing drivers. "Oh my, Zonie!" I shouted. "They're Vietnamese! They are going to box us in on the back road just like my dream. We must somehow turn around!"

"Hold on!" Zonie shouted as she spun her truck around.

Now heading in the opposite direction from the Vietnamese people tailgating us, Zonie got a good look at the driver as she floored her gas petal to outrun them.

Zonie sped back into town to the twenty-four-hour Marie's Pizza Parlor, where she could make a call.

As we flew into the parking lot in front of the pizza parlor, with her truck still running, Zonie jumped out, ran inside and began telling what had just happened. She asked to borrow their phone.

Zonie then called the Port Lavaca Sheriff's Department. After recounting what had just transpired, she demanded we get an escort back to Seadrift. She continued by warning the sheriff's office that our family knew where we were and if we did not arrive back to Seadrift safely, they would know it was because of the sheriff. They assured her an escort would come for us.

Still trembling, Zonie returned to her vehicle only to discover that the Vietnamese drivers had been circling on the highway behind us. Lana and I had been watching them, worrying about what they would do next. It seemed a long time as we sat there, waiting in terror for the police escort while watching the Vietnamese men circling like buzzards appearing to be searching for Zonie's truck. Finally the police arrived.

With the escort, we headed toward home. On the way down that lonely, empty dark stretch of road, we noticed a car backed into a pullover. As we passed, I recognized the car with the dress suits hanging in the back seat. I pointed it out to Zonie and said, "Paranoid, Sis? I don't think so. He may be from one of the government agencies."

As we arrived home, we were greeted with huge hugs and sighs of relief from our awake and waiting family. "I'm so thankful for that warning dream," I recounted to our mother.

Giving me one of her warm, loving hugs she was well-known for, Mother replied, "So am I." All full of gratitude that the Lord had kept us safe, we went to bed.

As we arose that next morning, my brother Rudy contacted a childhood friend of his and Billy Joe's. Their mutual friend was serving in the Secret Service to the president of the United States in Washington, D.C. Rudy was hoping his friend would speak to President Carter and get some help with a proper response from the authorities to find the murderers. Also, after all the events that had taken place, Rudy was hoping the president would order police protection for our family.

Likewise, I had served at the Texas state capitol as a lobbyist for the commercial seafood industry. Therefore, I called a friend who was the senator of Chambers County, Texas. The senator was surprised to learn it was my brother. He saw the news portraying mean, lazy, ignorant, dumb, aggressive, selfish Americans . . . something he knew I was not.

I said, "Please help find my brother's murderers. My family is being continually threatened by the Vietnamese."

"You know I will do what I can to help," the senator replied.

Confident in his promise, I said "Thank you!" then hung up the phone.

However, Rudy and Billy Joe's childhood friend had said, "I could not believe it was Billy Joe. Do *not* tell anyone you know me or that you have spoken with me because I could lose my job. Plus, if no one knows, I can do whatever is possible to help on this end."

"Thanks!" Rudy replied, also confident in his friend.

The following day the news reported the Vietnamese murderers had turned themselves in to authorities in Chambers County, the jurisdiction of my senator friend. I have often wondered if he had anything to do with their surrender, but I may never know. The Vietnamese killers were transported to the Port Lavaca County Jail.

The one who shot Billy Joe said he threw the handgun off the bridge at the bay in Seadrift. However, the rifle was confiscated and brought to the Port Lavaca County Jail, where the prisoners were held. Ironically it was reported that the rifle was later stolen from the county jail. No one knew who stole it or how. The handgun supposedly thrown off the bridge in Seadrift was never recovered. Both weapons used in a premeditated cold-blooded murder—missing!

It was also shared with us that on August 3, the day of Billy Joe's murder, one of the Vietnamese men's wives had rushed to the Seadrift police and reported that her husband and others had guns and were going to kill Billy Joe Aplin. We were told the man's wife tried to stop her husband and they got into a fight.

On the day of their surrender, one of the murderers had scratch marks like fingernails had clawed his face. However, in their concocted defense story, he said it was self-defense wounds from Billy Joe. The news played up that lie even though there were eyewitnesses of the factual events.

The police combed the waters under the Seadrift bridge to find the handgun used in the murder of Billy Joe Aplin, but to no avail. It was not there. Ironically, the rifle brought to assist in the murder of Billy Joe that was stolen from the Port Lavaca County Jail was also never recovered.

The sheriff and the jail administrator should have had the rifle locked up in the evidence room. However, they reported it was lying on a table in the jail and "someone stole it." Someone stole a murder weapon, a rifle, out of the Jail? A jail that was so secure Zonie had to call for them to open the locked doors?

Needless to say, our family was growing more and more disillusioned with our government, local police department, and the deceptive, lying news.

VIII

MEDIA ZOO

T he day of Billy Joe's funeral, the entire town of Seadrift closed their businesses. It was a sign of love and respect plus solidarity standing against such evil as murder.

Flowers packed the church as well as many laying roses one at a time on top of my brother, Captain Billy Joe Aplin's folded hands. Our parents—along with Billy Joe's widow and his three young children—entered the church, walking up that long aisle to Billy Joe's coffin. Grief such as this cannot be fathomed; needless loss of a child, a husband, a father, a brother, a friend. Bitter weeping and deep sobs were loudly heard, but ushers kept the media zoo outside the church doors. This was a solemn and private moment.

After church services, the drive to Seadrift's cemetery only brought more tears of reality and finality to our family. Media was again kept away from the immediate family. This was our private moment to grieve our loved one.

We held on to each other and our faith for strength. No more laughter and snickering for pranks by my older but youngest brother, no more hugs for Mother and Daddy, no more loving hugs and kisses for his wife and children, no more conversations about his dreams of being a ship pilot, no more . . . The finality of a cemetery. Only a huge concrete slab and headstone with his captain photo and a short description to detail the man we loved and admired so dearly.

After the funeral, my family and I had to go back to the Dallas, Texas, area, where we lived. My children were starting school, and the seafood market and employees needed me to keep things working properly. Big Net Shrimp Season was starting August 15, so my husband, Ronnie, had to go up the coast to get his boat and nets ready for his biggest season of the year. Life goes on; it does not stop for death or grief.

After we had left, I heard the KKK from a town about three hours away came to Seadrift. They said their reason for coming was to make sure the authorities returned my brother's shirt to our family.

I don't know how they were aware of anything except through the constant news reports. Their purpose sounded noble, but sadly their arrival became *fodder for the media zoo*. The focus was taken off of the facts and events within our country and twisted into another piece of propaganda to feed into the racist theme that the Vietnamese inhabitants and media were pushing. I am not, nor have I ever been, a racist. More distortions by the media, to weigh down my soul.

After I returned home, I made an appointment with my business accountant. My accountant was from the Philippines. At one time he ran for president of the Philippines. Having lost his race for president, he then ran to the United States to protect his life. He was excellent at keeping books, but his background was what first fascinated me.

My accountant called and said, "Annie, I need to speak with you privately. Please come to my home."

"OK," I replied with curiosity. We set a date and time for my visit. Upon arrival, I was warmly greeted into a lovely, Japanese-decorated home.

He pointed to his office and asked me to come in and take a seat. With a serious look of concern upon my accountant's face, he began sharing, "I have been working on a credit union for the Vietnamese."

He went on to say that the government had excellent benefits for this venture. His information was only disappointing and frustrating me more in what I was discovering as my out-of-balance government. What he said next did not surprise me.

"Crazy Law Gives Ex-Vietcong [Communists]
Job Preference Over U.S. Veterans"

"Annie, they [the Vietnamese] said for you to stop lobbying at the capitol or they would kill you." He thought he was doing me a favor with their message, but after what my family was already suffering, it only strengthened my fortitude.

"Tell them I said to go ahead and kill me. I will not stop! And I am going to fight against these evils as long and as hard as I can." He had delivered the message for the Vietnamese, and I sent my response. Therefore, we graciously parted.

THE BOMB

Big Net Shrimp Season beginning August 15, 1979, proved to be a very low-yield season. Big Net means the law does not limit the size of net you can pull behind your boat to harvest the shrimp. Most of the shrimp fishermen's income for the year is made during Big Net Season from August to December. However, that year—due to various weather issues—there were very few shrimp to be harvested.

My husband, Ronnie, had living quarters on his boat and lived on board during Big Net Season. Rarely did he drive the 250-mile trek home. He was a hardworking man and determined to try to catch what he could, while he could. However, his constant absence put an additional strain on me and our marriage.

While Ronnie was away on board his boat, I had our two young children, a thriving yet demanding business, employees, product to order and process, customers, a home to clean, clothes to launder, food to cook, and children to care for. I was an active member of the chamber of commerce and a state lobbyist. There was not any time for myself, but that was OK. My children and the business were my priority.

I not only managed the seafood market but I also processed a lot of the seafood. My hands would often be swollen from shrimp acid eating and infecting them. I was always a diligent worker, but now I needed to work harder to produce more income to compensate for the low shrimp yield.

Annie's Seafood Market, Richardson, Texas 1979

Ronnie and I married when I was eighteen and he was twenty years of age. Now we were in our middle twenties, but I often looked in my forties. The grief and stress were taking a toll on me and my health. As days and weeks went by, the grief over my brother and concern for my parents with long work hours were draining me. I continued crying out to the Lord for understanding because nothing made sense in my world.

One day I received the revelation that a house cat and a tiger are from the same species, but you cannot take a tiger from the jungle and put him in a house and tell him to act like a kitty cat no more than you can take a kitty cat and place it in a jungle and tell it to survive. I saw us as domesticated house cats, and the Vietnamese—due to survival in war—were the tigers. I often pondered, did the Vietnamese realize they no longer needed jungle warfare tactics? If they chose to, they could now live in peace. My thoughts were soon answered.

News reported that Defense Attorney Pat Mahoney Sr. accepted defending the two Vietnamese killers pro bono (free) after being asked by a San Antonio parish priest who he was close to.

The Texas State U.S. Justice Department would visit Seadrift to make sure things stayed calm. My family was fond of Mr. Alexander. They shared with him their concerns about the Vietnamese. Mr. Alexander agreed with their concerns and affirmed about 30 percent—maybe more—were Vietcong. Vietcong—the enemy our soldiers had been fighting—were now living among us, courtesy of our government and our hard-earned tax dollars.

Billy Joe was the one I first heard make the comment "Don't insult my intelligence" while speaking with me.

"What do you mean?" I asked.

Billy Joe responded, "Sis, the height of an insult to me is for someone to take advantage of my ignorance, and if they fail to do so, it's a direct insult to what intelligence I have." I pondered his statement a few minutes and I agreed. When Mr. Alexander visited with my family, he never insulted their intelligence. Even though he worked for the government, he appeared to be an honorable man.

Finally the day of trial for the Vietnamese killers arrived. As previously mentioned, these Vietnamese men were under refugee status and were not citizens. They were sponsored by the Catholic diocese and considered legal aliens. This status caused their trial to fall under different laws, just like the murder attempt on the water of Billy Joe and his family. We soon discovered again that the laws that affect American citizens are different than noncitizens.

The trial seemed to happen quickly, but to my family it dragged on. One day I accompanied Daddy into the courtroom to listen to the testimony of the Vietnamese man who pulled the trigger on the handgun. The courtroom was packed, so I sat in the row behind my dad. I was not aware there would be charts of entrance and exit wounds of my precious brother's body with physical detailed descriptions. Bits and pieces of every part of his entire body from the autopsy. Seeing these charts dredged to the surface the pain and suffering of my brother's death.

As his murderer was being questioned, he said he needed an interpreter because he didn't speak English. He testified through the interpreter things Billy Joe said verbally threatening him. When the prosecutor questioned him, he asked, "If you can't speak English and are using an interpreter, how can you know what Billy Joe Aplin was saying?" Silence.

The prosecutor then asked him to show how he was holding the handgun. The Vietnamese man stood up, stretched his arms out in front of him supporting the hold of the gun with his other hand. The prosecutor asked if Billy Joe's arms were up in surrender. "Yes. His arms were up and he turned to run," he responded. The prosecutor continued with descriptions of the angles of the gunshot and how it ripped through Billy Joe's aorta, how he hit the ground with blood filling up his body. At that point I had been watching my strong dad turning his head down, quietly crying, his shoulders shaking from the sobs of grief at seeing and hearing the horror his son had suffered. I had rarely seen my dad cry.

At the beginning of the trial, the judge had ordered no noise at all or he would clear the courtroom. At that point of seeing my dad silently weeping, I could not contain my grief. I grabbed my mouth and rushed out of the courtroom. Burying my head in the shoulder and my body in the arms of a friend, I began wailing with grief over Billy Joe and the pain of our dad.

Suddenly I felt intense heat on my back. I turned and looked up. It was several live news cameras with lights so bright and close they were hot on my back. Tears streaming down my face, I begged, "Go away! Please go away!" I then turned and buried my face from the media, which looked worse than vultures, and through sobs asked my friend, "Please make them go away." The courthouse police made them turn off their camera lights and back up.

I have always been private with grief and with my personal life. I have always preferred to grieve alone. Also, the news had been printing twisted truths and lies, making my family and all Americans look mean and the Vietnamese look pitiful. Because I had served as a lobbyist in the state of Texas, I knew most of the Texas legislators. Plus friends in the lobbying world. I did not want anyone seeing me distraught with grief. Nor did I want the news using my grief as a pawn, like they had done with my other siblings, to increase their deceptive narrative and their viewership.

As time went by, I once again gained my composure and waited outside the courtroom. The announcement was made that the jury was out deliberating the Vietnamese killers' fates.

I was approached by a newspaper reporter from the *Dallas Morning News*. He introduced himself and asked if he could have an interview. I would *never* give interviews to the media once I saw how they spun a story into a perceived lie. However, this reporter was different. I had read his articles, and they were true journalism. His stories always reported issues, incidents, events, and testimonies from various sources, but he never seemed to use his story for propaganda like others had done. This reporter only reported facts and allowed readers to come to their own conclusion. He appeared to be a true journalist.

I looked at him and said, "Yes, I will speak with you because you have been fair, with good reporting."

"Thank you," the reporter graciously responded.

He then continued, "You know the Vietnamese men are going to appeal. What are your thoughts about that?"

Everyone in the courtroom who had heard and seen the testimony *knew* the Vietnamese men were guilty of premeditated, cold-blooded murder, so the media was trying to get ahead of the story. All were convinced of the finding of premeditated murder.

I replied, "Once I had a huge oak tree in my front yard. One day it began dying. My husband and I thought it was moss on the limbs killing the old tree, so we scraped the moss. The tree continued to die, so we trimmed back the small limbs. Our tree was still dying, so we cut the massive limbs back to the trunk. Then a strong wind came and blew that huge old oak tree down and we saw it had root rot. The law can sentence the murderers to death. They can even blow Seadrift, Texas, off the face of the map, and it will not change things.

"We have root rot in this nation in Washington, D.C., and until that gets dealt with, you are only scraping moss and trimming branches."

Shortly after I gave my illustration to the reporter, word came out that the jury was back. "Wow, that was quick!" everyone thought. The media was everywhere covering the back of the courtroom.

The judge spoke. The Vietnamese men stood and faced the jury. The verdict was read: "We find . . . *not* guilty." Shock shot through the courtroom and through our hearts. It was on every news reporter's face as well as the faces of the Americans and the Vietnamese. The news reporters then rushed to the front of the courtroom to now encompass the Vietnamese men and get their response.

26 Rocky Mountain News   Sat., Nov. 3, 1979, Denver, Colo.

2nd Viet refugee acquitted of murder charge

SEGUIN, Texas (AP) — A state jury on Friday acquitted a young Vietnamese refugee on charges of killing a local fisherman during a "crab war" in the tiny coastal town of Seadrift.

The verdict came three hours and 20 minutes after the jury began deliberations on the murder charge against Nguyen Van Sau, 21, in the Aug. 3 dockside shooting of Billy Joe Aplin, 35. Sau could have faced a maximum 99-year prison sentence if convicted of murder. Sau's 20-year-old brother, Nguyen Van Chinh,

was acquitted Thursday on an instructed verdict by State District Judge Clarence Stevenson. Chinh also was charged with murder.

The shooting followed a dispute over local fishing customs, which hold that a fisherman does not put his crab traps in the same area another crabber has found to be "hot."

The trial was moved to Seguin, 90 miles inland, because of unrest among Seadrift's 1,400 residents.

When the verdict was announced, the victim's

older sister, Sarah Vincent, 41, wept and said, "My brother was killed in cold blooded murder and I believe they will murder all of us. I believe the Vietnamese will attempt to murder each and every one of my family. They own Seadrift now."

She added: "Never in our wildest dreams did we imagine they would be found not guilty."

Defense lawyer Pat Maloney said, "It's just magnificent ... Justice has so richly been served." He called the verdict "one of the most

reassuring events in my belief of the judicial system."

Sau wept briefly when an interpreter told him of the verdict. He smiled as he shook hands with each juror.

"He was very moved and very grateful and very happy," said interpreter Dr. Nguyen Van China.

Maloney, a San Antonio attorney who has donated his services, said the shooting occurred against the backdrop of racial hatred.

The pain from Billy Joe's death now compounded by the fury of his cold-blooded murderers going free only served to further my dad's growing concern for our nation. It was twice death. When you have a loved one murdered, you grieve their death. When you wait for justice to prevail but the murderers walk free, it's twice the death and twice the grief. This was not the America my dad was raised in, nor was it the America my parents taught us children about. None of my family could understand the events that transpired in that courtroom. The day following the release of the Vietnamese killers, my sister Noopy was at the supermarket in Seadrift buying groceries. At the same time, the sister of one of the murderers was in the supermarket checkout line in front of her. As they approached the checkout counter, where no one could see, the Vietnamese woman kicked Noopy.

TOP: Chinh Van Nguyen and Sau Van Nguyen walk through the Guadalupe County Courthouse in 1979. They were charged but acquitted of murder.

After the woman kicked my sister, Noopy began cursing the woman. My sister was full of grief from the loss of our brother and angry that the woman's brother was set free from murder. Unfortunately my sister fell into the woman's intimidating trap. No one saw that Noopy had been kicked. It looked like Noopy was cursing at the woman because her brother was free, not because the woman instigated it by attacking Noopy. The woman did this to make herself look pitiful and my sister look mean. Exactly how the news had been spinning the lies.

The day after the trial, newspaper reporters were still everywhere. One heard my sister cursing and rushed over to get the story. Noopy shouted, "She kicked me!" At that point the Vietnamese woman could not contain her laughter. However, that news reporter told the truth in his article when he stated "it was no laughing matter."

A few days later, the threatening phone calls started again at my parents' home.

Their phone would ring. "Hello?"

"Five more to die! Five more to die!" the Vietnamese would shout then hang up.

No one tapped my parents' phone line to catch the terrorist. But all of my family that lived, worked, and had businesses in Seadrift was always on high alert. I even had to be constantly watching due to the threats sent to me through my accountant.

One day on the bay, Noopy was running her crab traps when suddenly Vietnamese boats came from behind the small islands, rushing toward her. Knowing how they had attacked her brother and his family, she frantically floored her boat, heading toward shore. Noopy looked back and saw the Vietnamese boats were gaining on her. At their approaching speed, she did not have time to get to the docks to safety. She immediately headed toward an oil platform, where she knew other Americans were.

Noopy pulled up yelling, "Help me! Help me! The Vietnamese are chasing me, trying to kill me!" As the men helped to secure her boat and brought her onto the platform, the Vietnamese boats turned away.

Once on the platform, it appeared Noopy was having a heart attack from the terror. The men called a helicopter, which LifeFlighted her to the nearest hospital, where she was promptly treated.

When our parents and we siblings heard what happened to Noopy, we were even more aware of the Vietnamese's intent to kill us all to take over the seafood industry in Seadrift, Texas. After all, Billy Joe's murderers went free from cold-blooded murder, and it emboldened the rest of the Vietnamese clan. They now knew they could terrorize, murder, and intimidate with absolutely no consequences and no reprisal. They knew there would be no reprisal from my family because we were law-abiding citizens. No reprisal from the government because they were allowed to walk free from murder. No reprisal from the news because they were spinning everything to pity the Vietnamese and make Americans look like selfish, mean bullies. No consequences at all. What would stop them from taking over?

A Spanish Reporter from the *New York Times* approached the front door of Doc's home. He knocked on the door, and Doc answered. "May I help you?" Doc asked.

The very polite man introduced himself and said he was a reporter for the *New York Times*. "Will you allow me to interview you, Mr. Aplin?" the reporter asked.

"I'm sorry, but I do not give interviews anymore. All the news writes is distortions and lies," Doc replied.

The gentleman spoke very compellingly. "I *promise*, if you allow me an interview, I will write all of the facts and leave nothing out."

Doc peered into the man's eyes and felt he could see authenticity and commitment. He opened the door and invited him in.

Doc offered the reporter a cup of coffee, then pointed to the sofa for him to have a seat. Coffee in one hand with a pen in the other and pad on the coffee table, the reporter said, "OK, Mr. Aplin, let's begin." Doc shared our family's and the town's heart-wrenching stories from the influx of the Vietnamese refugees to that present time in 1979.

At the end of the interview, the reporter was overwhelmed by the truth-supported facts of all the events. The reporter's story complete, they shook hands and bid each other good-bye.

When the article came out in the *Times*, Doc was livid with fury for allowing himself to be deceived by the reporter. The story was far from the truth.

Doc's phone rang; he answered. The voice on the other end was the reporter's. Doc began telling him off for the trash The news had printed. When Doc finally calmed down, the reporter said, "Doc, I am sorry. I turned in my story with all of the supporting data like I promised. My editor called me into his office and said, 'This is not what we are printing. This is.' My copy lay in pieces on the floor. I pleaded with the editor, but it fell on deaf ears. Doc, I'm sorry, but I wanted you to know that was not my story."

"Now you can see how we have been treated by the news. They don't seem to care about the truth or facts," Doc replied.

The reporter responded, "I know, Doc. It surprised me! Now I know why you don't want to give interviews. Again, I am sorry." They bid each other good-bye and hung up the phone.

After the failed attempt on our sister's life, Doc would not run his commercial crab traps. He had been concerned about going out upon the water. All of my siblings and their children were gravely concerned. However, in time, they had to earn a living, so all went back to work.

Doc was still shipping Texas blue crabs all over the USA. Billy Joe's widow offered to help Doc's daughter, Linda, run his traps. The crab traps had been sitting a long time, and my brother's widow wanted to help. They loaded the boat with crab bait and very cautiously headed out onto the bay.

While running the trap line, Linda took the long pole with a hook on the end, slid it under the buoy that held the line to the crab trap, jerked the pole, and grabbed the line to pull the crab trap on board. Once the trap was pulled out of the water, chills of horror went through their spines. Attached to the trap was a *bomb*! They carefully pulled the trap on board, into the boat, and quickly headed to shore.

Once back at Doc's home, the sight of seeing the bomb attached to his trap was terrifying. Doc knew the bomb was designed to kill him but almost took his daughter and sister-in-law's lives. More evidence that the Vietnamese were going to keep killing to take over the seafood industry in Seadrift, Texas. Doc took a photo of the bomb, then put the trap with the attached device in his backyard. Suddenly the police pulled up at Doc's home. They informed my brother that they heard about the bomb on one of his traps and ordered Doc to give them the trap. After all of the unusual events that had happened to our family—such as one of our brother's murder weapons going missing from the county jail, Doc did not trust the police and said, "No. It's my property, and you are not taking it."

Bomb on Crab Trap, Seadrift, Texas 1979

The policeman then replied, "Yes, I am confiscating it, and don't try to stop me!"

Without a warrant, the policeman walked onto Doc's property and took the crab trap with the bomb affixed to it, then left. What the police were not aware of was that Doc had already taken photos of the trap as evidence.

In the photos, one could see that the bomb appeared to be made out of railroad flares. There was a metal line that had been tied under the buoy down to the bomb so that when the gaff hook jerked the rope, it would detonate the bomb. *Kaboom!* However, since Doc had not run his traps in a couple weeks, electrolysis had eaten through the line and made it ineffective. All of us were rejoicing and giving praise to the Lord for His intervention. Once more my family had escaped death at the hands of the Vietnamese.

We were a strong, hardworking, and proud family with a steadfast Christian faith. My parents and siblings had a resolve that these murderers and terrorists were not going to frighten them out of their homes or businesses. We were all determined to continue forward even in the face of continuing death threats. Seadrift was home to most of my family. It's where our parents raised their children and many of their grandchildren. It was where many of us went to school, met our spouses, played baseball with our dad (who could outrun us all), ate Sunday dinners, had holiday gatherings, went fishing, did gardening, worked. It was *home*. They were determined not to be threatened or bullied out of their home.

I was the youngest child and lived a long way away in Plano, Texas. As mentioned earlier, I was a business owner at the age of nineteen and became a state lobbyist for the commercial seafood industry in my early twenties. However at this time, my beautiful and productive seafood market on Central Expressway in Richardson, Texas, was hurting from the slowdown in the shrimping industry. However, the threats by the Vietnamese had not yet been directed at the shrimping industry. The threats had been directed at me personally not to speak to the Texas legislators but not to commercial shrimp fishermen.

My husband, living on his boat, worked free from the terror plaguing my family. Emotionally I was never free from the pain of loss and my family being terrorized. I often cried out, "No more, Lord! Please do not let anyone else die!" Every time a relative called, I would hold my breath until I heard all were well and alive.

One day during the time Billy Joe's murderers were set free, I was watching a news broadcast on which Iranians were burning American flags on American soil. They were shouting horrible things about my country, and no one was punished for burning our precious flag. My heart was deeply burdened over this sight.

Since the founding of the United States of America, every generation of my family has served in the military and fought for and/or under the American flag. One of our ancestral grandfathers through my grandmother, Clark Aplin, came over on the Pilgrim ship the *Swan*. It is the same ancestral grandfather to President Thomas Jefferson. My dad's mother was half Cherokee and my mother's Grandmother Peacock was also Cherokee. Our family has fought in every war for this nation and protecting other nations. Our roots run deep. My family was true American patriots and loved our nation.

As I observed the news, watching our precious flag being burned by Iranians in California on American soil, a poem rose within me and I penned these words:

"AMERICA'S RIGHTS"

How can we let them burn our Red, White, and Blue?
How can people discern whether you are them or they are you?

Do you still cross your heart when you give your vows?
Do tears fill your eyes as she waves gracefully giving bows?

What has happened to our National Anthem that we all used to sing? Where is our Pride and Dignity when we hear our Freedom Bells Ring?

"America the Beautiful" is all we used to hear. When did it darken, along with the fading cheers?

Where are any more leaders with a strong backbone and full of pride? Instead of projected images making laws full of holes in which they can Hide.

And what about our Grand Lady who watches over this land so Free? Our Forefathers cleared this ground out of the wilderness to ease things for you and me.

America! Land of Milk and Honey! Where humanitarianism is on the rise!

These words have echoed around the world giving parasites an entering disguise.

Do we idly sit and complain about the destruction within our land so free?
Or do we claim "AMERICA'S RIGHTS" and ban her rotting debris?

If the Statue of Liberty could cry, she would flood the harbor in which she stands,
Tears for immortality, corruption, and gross injustice flowing throughout her land.

"Dear God!" I cry in my despair. "Give me strength to face another day!
Wake our country up to its woes and cares; open our eyes before it is too late!"

1979, by Annie Aplin

JOSIE AND DALE'S DEATH

The rest of 1979, Thanksgiving, and Christmas came and went with much grief and lots of concern for each other. My parents continued getting threatening phone calls. Most of my family was now carrying guns to protect themselves on the water. Everyone had the resolve that the terrorists would not drive them out of their homes. The government was still doing nothing.

In February 1980, six months after Billy Joe's death, I received a phone call saying, "Josie and Dale went out on the water yesterday and have not made it back yet." Again, fear of the worse gripped my soul.

Josie was my parents' sixth child, and Dale was her husband.

It was winter; therefore, my husband's Big Net Season was over. He was at home with the children and me. Ronnie begrudgingly helped me work in the seafood market. He also did not enjoy taking care of the children or any other job related to our home or my business, but he did them. After the news of Josie and Dale being missing, we closed the doors on the seafood market to begin the long drive from Plano to Seadrift, Texas.

Along the way we stopped at my husband's grandmother's for what became a short visit. It was my birthday. All of my husband's family was there to surprise me. I received many birthday gifts, but my favorite was Grandmother's homemade crocheted pillow and my mother-in-law's crocheted blanket. It was a wonderful time, but in the back of my mind I was waiting for the call that my sister and brother-in-law were safe. Finally, the call came; it was Doc's daughter, Regina.

"They found the boat today, and it doesn't look good," Regina said.

"OK," I answered, as I held back the onslaught of tears.

Hanging up the phone, covering my mouth, I began running toward the front door to go outside to cry. Grandmother was old, and I did not want to upset her with my grief. However, as I ran toward the door, the floor suddenly greeted me as I collapsed. My husband scooped me up in his arms and asked, "What did Regina say?"

As he held me, through strangling tears I repeated those dreadful words: "They found their boat today, but it doesn't look good."

"I've got to go to look for Josie and Dale" I told my husband. "I understand. We will go in the morning," he replied.

"No, we have to leave now. I have to get there and look for them!" I exclaimed.

"I know, but its dark outside. You can't do anything until daylight," Ronnie reasoned.

"Maybe not, but I must get there now. Please," I pleaded.

"OK, we will go," My husband replied with shrugged shoulders in surrender.

Ronnie knew there was nothing we could do at night, but I was only thinking of Josie and Dale. Where were they? Were they on an island freezing from the cold? All I knew is my sister and brother-in-law were missing, and I needed to go be with my family and help find them.

It was in the middle of the night when my husband and I arrived at my parents' home. With strong resolve, all were hoping when morning came that we would find Josie and Dale—alive.

I asked, "What happened?" They began recounting the story from two days earlier:

Josie and Dale were going to work to run their traps. Their crab trap line was across the bay about twenty-five miles by boat, near Aransas Pass Game Preserve. Before they left, the weather reported a cold front was on its way. Mother asked Josie not to go, but Josie said, "We have to go to work, Mother. We need the money."

Josie's oldest sister, Noopy, drove to the docks and also asked her and Dale not to go until the cold front passed through. Cold fronts can bring freezing winds and high waves on the bay. However, this concern was secondary in Noopy's mind to them traveling so far with the threat of the Vietnamese, and in bad weather.

Josie comforted her sister: "It's OK, Noopy. If the cold front comes through, then Dale and I will stay in a cabin on one of the islands." Noopy was aware that the bay was dotted with small islands, and some islands had cozy hunting cabins on them.

Satisfied with their plan for protection, Noopy hugged her sister and said, "Be careful, sis! I love you!"

She then turned to her brother-in-law and said, "I know you will take care of her, Dale, and not let anything happen to her. Stay safe!"

That morning, Josie and Dale had been doing their daily devotional reading before heading to work. Bible still in hand, Josie closed it, placing it back onto the front seat of their car. As they boarded their boat, heading out to sea, Josie turned back, waving good-bye to her eldest sister, who was still standing on the bank waving at her. Noopy kept waiting as their boat sped away . . . watching . . . wanting to protect her younger sister from the dread she felt deep within her soul.

As the boat was going out of sight, Noopy tried shaking the impending sense of doom, saying to herself, "Dale is a marine. He would never let anyone or anything harm Josie." Little did Noopy know that this would be her final "I love you" and "Good-bye" to her precious sister and brother-in-law.

As evening approached, Josie and Dale were not back. Doc did not know the conversation they had earlier with Noopy. He became fearful for their safety and called the coast guard.

That evening Doc went to our parents' home to announce Josie and Dale were not back from crabbing. Noopy was there and shared, "They said they would stay overnight at a camp on one of the islands." Relief flooded everyone's minds at that announcement. All was well.

Early the following morning a knock came at Doc Aplin's door. He opened it to find the coast guard on his front porch. Suddenly he remembered that he had forgotten to call them to stop the search.

As Doc began to apologize to the coast guard, they interrupted him, saying, "We could not find them or their boat."

Troubled and confused, not wanting to believe what the coast guard was saying, Doc asked, "What? What do you mean? You can't find them or their boat?"

"We have been searching since first light, and they are nowhere to be found. It's as though they just vanished. It's very odd," the coast guard replied and continued, "We should have been able to find them, the boat, debris from the boat, *something*! We have thoroughly searched every area you reported, and we have found nothing!"

Seadrift Harbor Master,
B.T. Aplin, 1980

With one hand on his hip, Doc ran the other hand through his hair as he often did when in distress. Trying to mentally grasp the coast guard's unusual report, he asked, "Are you continuing to search?"

"Yes. We are expanding our search," the coast guard replied. "We will keep you posted."

Doc shook their hands, thanking them, then they turned and walked away. With a heavy heart, Doc had to go to his already grief-stricken parents' home to prepare them for what might be the worst. He then had his daughter, Regina, begin calling all his siblings to give us the news that Josie and Dale were missing.

That night, some of Mother and Daddy's close friends came over to pray and encourage them—all hoping to soon find both Josie and Dale alive. Late that night as my parents' friends were driving back home past the waterfront, they saw what appeared to be a large boat pulling a small boat behind it. The ladies pulled their car over, shining their

76

headlights onto the dark water to see if the smaller vessel might be Josie and Dale's boat.

As soon as their lights shone onto the water, the Seadrift Police pulled up, commanding them to leave, *now*! Surprised by the orders, they obeyed the police but were puzzled at why they demanded them to leave. There was no curfew in town or at the waterfront. This was all strangely puzzling to the ladies.

The following morning, Josie and Dale's crab fishing boat was found capsized in shallow water near our oldest brother's docks in Seadrift. Our dad was harbormaster and immediately called the coast guard upon the discovery of his daughter and son-in-law's boat.

As the area was examined by the authorities, they found absolutely no debris nearby, nor had any been discovered in their extensive search of the bay. The only thing they found was Dale's fishing boots, which were standing upright in the mud by the boat. The scene appeared very staged to the authorities as well as my family. However, the media vultures swarming the area began the theme of Dale killing his wife, dumping the boat, and swimming away in the frigid bay waters. My entire family knew this was not true. Dale loved Josie with his whole life and was very protective of her. At the discovery of the boat, with no bodies or debris, the coast guard and other volunteers began the expanded hook search. This type of search is done by fastening *huge* fishing hooks across a metal bar and dragging it through the mud across the bottom of the water to see if it will hook into the flesh of their bodies. A horrible thought and an even more intimidating sight for my family and me to see.

That night at Mother and Daddy's home, no one had remembered it was my birthday. However, to me that meant nothing. My only thought was getting out upon the bay to assist in the ongoing search for my sister and brother-in-law.

About an hour before daylight, I asked if someone would take me out into the freezing weather to look for Josie and Dale. My husband said, "Baby, it's still dark outside. You have to wait for daylight."

"I can't sit here until daylight knowing they are out there somewhere in this cold weather. They could freeze if we don't hurry and find them!" I shared with extreme concern.

My niece Regina's husband, Jerry, said, "I will take you. Let's go!"

"Great! Thank you, Jerry!" I replied as I hurried to put on my coat and boots.

Jerry Jeter and wife Regina (Aplin) Jeter, Pastor

My husband and daddy both felt good about me going with Jerry because he not only was an expert boatman but he also carried a gun for protection. After all, Mother and Daddy's terrorizing phone threats of "Five more to die!" had never stopped.

Jerry and I quickly headed for the docks. Upon arrival, the first light of dawn was breaking. As Jerry prepared the boat with fuel and supplies, I saw a longtime family friend standing by the boat ramp. He had his arms folded with a fixed stare out upon the bay.

I walked over, and as we greeted each other, I asked, "What are you looking at?"

"The place where they found your sister's boat," our friend replied as he pointed to the water. He continued with great disdain, "There is *no way* that boat has been there!"

"How do you know?" I asked.

"I flew over this entire area several times. That boat was not there. It was not anywhere!" Our friend owned a private plane. He had been helping in the search-and-rescue operation.

"Maybe you missed it," I replied.

"No! There is *no way* I could have missed it! You can see *everything* from the air, and it's in a shallow area sticking out of the water. No, it wasn't there!" he stated emphatically.

"Thank you for helping! Jerry and I are heading out to look for them," I replied.

I jumped on board the boat in the front, with Jerry at the back. Starting up the motor, he aimed his boat out into the frigid cold upon the waves.

My tears were masked by the freezing winds blowing into our faces, along with the spray of the icy water as the waves broke over the bow of the boat. The harsh weather only strengthened our determination that we *must* find Josie and Dale quickly!

Every time something bobbed on the water as the boat approached it, I would brace myself at the thought that this could be my precious sister or brother-in-law. As Jerry took me across the bay, from island to island, we shouted "Josie! Dale! Josie! Dale!" I continued to pray, "Lord, please let us find them alive."

After several hours of searching the bay at high speeds, our only find was wood floating on the water. We could find no sight of anyone on the islands, plus there was no sign of a fire being built. Suddenly we saw a boat in the distance rushing toward us. It was my dad and my husband, Ronnie.

As Daddy's boat approached beside us, my husband reached his hand down to pull me up onto Daddy's boat. As I reached up and looked into my husband's sad eyes, I asked, "Did you find them?"

"Yes, Josie" he replied with a deep sigh.

I then asked the question that Ronnie's demeanor was expressing: "Is she dead?"

"Yes," he replied as he broke down in tears.

I hugged my husband, then went immediately into the wheelhouse of Daddy's boat to comfort him and myself. As I walked into the cabin, Daddy and I held each other in a warm embrace. I found it odd, but my Dad appeared to be happy.

Through a look of sorrow with tears, Daddy pulled away from our embrace and joyfully announced, "We found my girl! She isn't lost anymore." With his arm still around the shoulders of his baby girl, we stood in silence as he turned his boat back toward shore. The only thing that could be heard above the roar of the engine was mine and my Dad's sobbing. On the long journey back across the water, I gathered strength, looked up, and asked, "Where did they find her, and is she OK, Daddy?"

For me to ask "Is she OK?" may sound strange, but with the knowledge of her being in the water or on an island, she could have been eaten by sharks, fish, many things in the water. On the islands, there were snakes and wild boars that could have hurt her. Daddy knew I was wanting to know if she was in one piece.

Tears were flowing down his rugged, unshaven face, almost frozen by the icy winter air, as he explained "They found her body floating in the water about ten miles away from the docks, but we have her!"

"Have they found Dale yet?" I asked. "No, not yet," Daddy replied.

As we arrived back at Mother and Daddy's home, Rudy arrived from Port O'Conner, where the coast guard had brought Josie's body. Rudy sat down, and with a sigh, he recounted the events that had just transpired: "As I arrived at the port, I started walking through the gates to the docks where the helicopter brought Josie. An armed guard held a gun on me and said he would shoot if I walked any further. I looked at him and said, 'That's my sister they just brought in, so shoot! I'm not stopping.' He put his gun down and let me continue to pass. It was horrible; they dropped Josie on the dock like she was only a sack of potatoes. I went over to her to see how she looked because the mayor said she had drowned, but that's ridiculous! Josie's mouth was clamped shut so tight she had bitten through her bottom lip. No way did Josie drown with her mouth shut!"

"Was she in one piece, Rudy? Had crabs or fish been chewing on her?" someone asked.

"No. She looked OK." Seeing our parents' distress, Rudy did not say anything else. No one did.

The coast guard went to Doc Aplin's home to formally inform him that they had recovered his sister's body. They knocked on the door. Doc opened it and invited them into his home, saying, "I've already heard about Josie."

Doc pointed to his couch and the coast guardsmen sat down. They began explaining, "Josie and Dale had gone twenty-five miles one direction across the bay and the boat was found the opposite direction at Seadrifts Harbor in shallow water with nothing on the boat except Dale's boots sunken upright in the mud. Then Josie's body was found ten miles in an absolutely different direction." They continued, "An oyster fisherman found her floating facedown. She had a yellow heavy raincoat on with an air bubble in the back of the raincoat floating her like a life jacket. It was as though someone had popped the back of the coat to catch air to help her float." At the end of the coast guard's recounting of the events, they shook their heads and added, "There is *no way* your sister could have been in that part of the bay from the boat. There are many reefs and shallow areas. She could not have been swept there by the wind; someone would have had to have placed her there."

As they were leaving, Doc said, "Thank you for looking for my sister. Please continue to search for Dale."

"We are and we will!" the coast guardsmen affirmed.

The following day, funeral arrangements for Josie's funeral were being made even though Dale was still missing, and the search continued.

Josie's only child was a thirteen-year-old daughter named Tammy. Therefore, our mother had to make all of the decisions for Josie's funeral. She first decided to have an open-coffin funeral since her body was intact. Josie was thirty years old, intellectually brilliant, and just as kind and beautiful as she was intelligent. Josie loved children and would sing to my son and daughter just like she always sang to me. Her favorite color was pink, and Mother chose my sister Margarette and I to pick out her clothes and coffin.

Margrette Aplin

My husband drove Margrette and me into Port Lavaca to go shopping for Josie's clothes. That part, though painful, was the easiest because the time came to bring the clothes to the funeral home, to our sister, Josie.

With apprehension we went inside. We viewed the coffins, then agreed on one we thought Josie would like. It matched her pink outfit we had just purchased.

Two morticians were working that day, one older and one younger. The younger mortician walked over to me as I awaited them dressing Josie to bring her out for viewing.

"Annie Aplin?" the young mortician asked. "Yes," I replied.

With a joyful twinkle in his eye, he reminded me of his name and said, "Don't you remember me? We attended Port Lavaca High School together."

"No. I'm so sorry. I don't remember you," I whispered through my grief and anxious anticipation of seeing my deceased sister.

The young man continued trying to jog my memory and have a school reunion in the funeral home waiting parlor. My despair over Josie was enormous, but this young man could not see it. I was good at hiding my grief. Soon after his failed attempts to help my memory of him, he excused himself and departed.

My sister Margarette and I were the two youngest of my parents' eight children. Margarette was two years older than me. We were all very close. Margarette had a mental breakdown after the murder of our brother and the terrorizing threats from the Vietnamese. Now she sat in silence and could not speak at all from the intense pain over Josie. I worried about what would happen to Margarette once we saw our precious sister. After all, Josie was only a year older than Margrette and they were very close.

The time came that the double doors were opened, and they said, "Your sister is ready; you can come in now."

Margarette, Ronnie, and I—all holding each other—approached Josie's coffin. "Oh, no, that won't do! She was *beautiful*, and she looks horrible!" I emphatically stated.

I then looked up at the young mortician and said, "You must remove *all* of this makeup. The colors are all wrong. Plus, why is her hair pulled back and tucked under her head? Josie always wore it full and wavy around her face."

I had not given the young man a chance to answer even one question before I shot another question at him. Our shock over how we could not recognize our sister was overwhelming to Margarette and me.

Patiently the young mortician said, "I can't remove the makeup. We can put additional over it. As far as her hair, we can work on that as well."

"No, I will do it," I replied. I felt no one knew Josie's face and hair as well as my sister Margarette and me.

"OK. I will be right back," the young mortician replied as he hurried out of the room.

Moments later the young man returned with makeup, a curling iron, and a hair comb in hand. "Here, Annie. I will hold them for you."

With Margarette and my husband standing at the foot of Josie's coffin looking on, I began the labor of love of carefully styling her hair and applying her makeup—properly.

As I was styling the front of Josie's hair, I noticed evenly spaced chunks of skin missing across her forehead. Then as I placed makeup on her face, I saw the deep bite marks on her bottom lip, remembering Rudy's description of how he found her. I thought back to how Josie would always bite her lip when she was in pain or under stress. There were other marks and bruises on my sister's face, and I pointed them out to the young mortician as I discovered them.

The young man responded, "I Know. There are also bruises, one on each side of her waist." Pointing to the area of the bruises. "And in other areas," he added.

With a huge sigh, I continued with the chore at hand, trying to help my sister look better. There was nothing I could do to make whatever caused Josie's bruising and pain go away, but I could help her look more presentable. I pressed through, despite my agonizing grief.

Finally I completed the task. Looking up from the top of my sister's coffin toward the foot where Ronnie and Margrette stood, I asked Margarette, "How does she look?"

"Much better," Margarette replied. My husband agreed.

At that moment, the elder mortician asked me to step into his office. He needed to give me Josie's personal belongings they had removed from her body.

"One man's motion watch. One . . ." the older mortician counted. I couldn't hear past "one man's motion watch." It was Dale's, but Josie had it on. The watch had to be vigorously shaken to keep time, but it had only recently stopped. This truly puzzled me.

I pointed this out to the mortician and was stunned by what he said. "You need to tell your parents to pull your sister's autopsy report, because she did not drown. Plus she has not been dead that long."

Puzzled by his statement, I asked, "What do you mean she hasn't been dead that long?"

"Because I know she hasn't. I work on drowning victims all the time, and she did not drown and has not been dead that long! Also a person does not bleed and bruise once they are dead. She received those bruises while she was alive," he exclaimed.

I was not wanting to believe that Josie had also been murdered, so I reasoned, "Maybe her body didn't deteriorate as fast because the water was so cold."

"It doesn't matter. I have worked on drownings in cold water. I'm telling you, your parents need to pull your sister's autopsy report and report it to the police," he replied in a demanding demeanor.

"Report it to the police?" I thought. "More false news reports? More media vultures hanging over my family's shoulders and in our faces while my sister and brother-in-law's murderers go free? *Report it? How? To whom?* Pull the autopsy report? Are you kidding?" These thoughts were flooding my mind.

Mother had asked for a different coroner for Josie than the one who autopsied Billy Joe because the coroner messed up his autopsy. However, the authorities used the same coroner.

My thoughts were racing. "Who can I report it to? Oh, my, what about Mother and Daddy? This will kill them. They are hanging on by a thread as it is. It's one thing to know a death is an act of God and another when it's death at the hands of a murderer. Plus, Josie had numerous signs of torture. Oh God, please help me!" This and more raced through my mind as I sat with the mortician. I was unsure of how much of this was rehearsed only in my mind, or had I blurted it out through my pain?

I had pondered if Josie and Dale were murdered, and this confirmed it. What was I to do with this information? How would reporting it bring Josie or Dale back? Our government and judicial system had shown there was no protection or justice for Americans. With this heavy weight upon my young shoulders, I thanked the mortician, gathered my sister's things, and left. Per the mortician's instruction, I secretly ordered my sister's autopsy report.

Valentine's Day was the date chosen for Josie's funeral. Dale's body was still missing, but the search continued in progress. We had hoped Dale would be found in time to be buried together with Josie on Valentine's Day.

The church was full. Our family filed through to the front of the sanctuary to see our precious sister, mother, daughter, aunt, cousin, and friend one final time. As Rudy passed by me, he whispered, "Thank you sis. She looks so much better than when I saw her at the coast guard docks." That statement alone by my brother settled within my soul that the sacrifice was worth it.

After services, Josie was then loaded into a golden hearse and brought to the cemetery in Seadrift to be buried near our brother Billy Joe. At the end of graveside services, all of the Aplin family went back to our parents' home. Mother was sixty-six years old and Daddy was sixty-three years of age at the time. Our entire family was deeply concerned that grief would give our parents heart failure and we would lose them. So we hid our enormous pain as much as possible and took comfort in each other's loving embrace.

Strangely but refreshingly, there were no obvious news reporters at Josie's funeral. Oddly enough, when the news of her and Dale missing was aired, it was very quickly quieted from the major news networks. We assumed the government was keeping it "hushed" to keep a lid on the potential outbreak of violence. Most citizens believed Josie and Dale were also murdered.

The coast guard and friends continued searching for Dale's body another two weeks but to no avail. The news and gossip mill began whispering that Dale may have killed Josie and fled. Our family was confident that he did not.

Ronnie and I had to return home and reopen my business in Richardson, Texas. Our bills were enormous. Big Net Season was a loss, so the market had to keep paying all of the bills or we would lose everything. However, with the intense grief from all the deaths and concern for my family's safety, my heart was not in continuing to grow a booming business. Ronnie didn't understand that I was just trying to breathe and take one day at a time, hoping for no more phone calls. The long workdays and my crying when we were alone was taking a toll on my marriage.

The entire time after the mortician's information, I continued waiting and wondering if I should tell our mother and daddy what he had shared about Josie's death and the timing. I felt helpless. What good would it do to tell my parents? Again I wondered, who would be prosecuted? What additional lies would the media run with? How much more pain could my parents take? In the end, I chose not to tell anyone about the mortician's disclosure but to keep the horrific information concerning Josie to myself. Keeping this secret also took its toll on my emotions that I was now having to bottle up for my husband's benefit.

Shortly after the failed search for Dale's body, the calls from the Vietnamese men to my parents' home began again. "More to die! More to die!" These words haunted my parents because there was absolutely nothing they could do to stop them.

In addition to the threatening calls, for six months my parents had been receiving calls from Americans around the country. These concerned citizens were expressing their condolences and giving information on how they too had been terrorized. They shared that the government did nothing to protect them. These informative calls to my parents revealed that small trucking business was interfered with for a Vietnamese takeover. Numerous reports came from American citizens concerning the illegal behavior of these legal aliens.

These reports had once strengthened my parents' resolve to not give up and not give in to these terrorist tactics. They were not helping now. So many children and failed attempts by the Vietnamese to do them harm . . . now two dead and one missing.

My parents were strong and not cowards, but continuing to be victimized by the Vietnamese and our government not stopping them was too much. Nowhere to turn. My Mother turned to the only source she trusted, and that was the Lord. With no place to run, she fell to her knees strengthened by the power of Jesus Christ, her Lord and Savior, who was her shelter. She cried out, and resolve came suddenly.

In final surrender, Mother began going to all of her children and adult grandchildren begging them to move. "I can't lose any more children! Please *move*! Let them have everything! I don't want to bury any more children; it's not worth it! Please move!" With these words she compelled our dad and all of her children to let go of everything they had worked for—their homes, their businesses, their land Daddy now farmed, their boats, everything of financial value, plus their amazing friends like family.

Mother was often called a saint because of her Christian faith, moral values, and love for others. Everyone could see the intense grief was taking a toll on her life, and no one wanted to see her hurting. Our family was a strong and determined people who did not want to give in to the Vietnamese terrorists and run for our lives, but what could we do? Without protection from our government and judicial system, all everyone in Seadrift could do was flee. One by one, all of Mother and Daddy's children agreed to move. But where?

APLIN FAMILIES FLEEING
FOR THEIR LIVES

My brother Rudy lived in southern Louisiana. He asked our parents to move to Grand Chenier, where he and his family lived. Our mother and daddy concluded that the Cajuns in Louisiana would *never* allow the lawlessness to go on that Texas had allowed. With this as their final decision, they spoke with each of their children and adult grandchildren about where they would go. Some said they could find a place further south in Texas, others further north up the coast in Texas, and a few said they would move to Louisiana and Florida.

Our entire family was being splintered by having to flee, but they felt safe again in the hope that everyone would stay alive.

The Vietnamese had been terrorizing people for years to take over the bay and the seafood industry in Seadrift, Texas. Mr. Aplin had begged the government for years to step in and teach the Vietnamese the American way of life, but to no avail. It took the deaths of several of my parents' children, with several failed attempts to murder others, with no reprisal from the American government. The Vietnamese finally succeeded in the takeover of the bay and the seafood industry in Seadrift, Texas.

Thirty family members, leaving eight businesses plus homes and families, fled to other areas of the country to protect our mother and daddy from dying of grief mixed with fear. Since my family had to abandon their homes and businesses, they started at the bottom again. Unlike the Vietnamese, who had enormous government support. Vietnamese could get low-interest small-business loans. They also received government-matched employment pay to businesses that would hire them. In addition to other free assistance—none of which was available to my family.

Even though we were United States citizens, we had now become refugees within our own country and Prey for the Enemy.

ANNIE AND CHILDREN
HELD HOSTAGE

My desire to continue building the seafood market was gone. My enormous drive was diminished. Therefore, Ronnie and I sold the seafood market and moved to Austin, Texas, where I could lobby and expose the Vietnamese plight. I would like to add, not all Vietnamese were terrorists. Not all wanted to harm. Many just wanted a free life and were learning how to live in a country free of communism and war. Yes, many did take advantage of our generous social system, but again, our government's fault for not having tighter regulations. However, there were numerous terrorist Vietnamese/Vietcong among us.

Not long after our move to Austin, I began receiving threats. I never forgot my accountant's warning that the Vietnamese said they would kill me if I lobbied the state legislature. I was not afraid. At this point I was furious over what had been happening to my family, unchecked by our government.

Shortly after moving to Austin, a Doberman began taking up residence at my home with my little outdoor terrier. One day as I was getting into my car, the Doberman jumped in like it was wanting to go with me. I am allergic to dog dander, so I made it get out. When I arrived back home, the Doberman was still there at my front door but had a note hanging around its neck saying, "Put your dog up!" It wasn't my dog, so I ignored it. The next day the Doberman was again at my front door, vomiting up pink stuff. It ran away and I never saw the Doberman again.

Our home was located on a cliff. Access into the house was from only two directions, through the woods on the side or from the front. Soon after the dog's disappearance, early in the morning, I stepped out onto my side deck to view the hills while sipping a cup of steaming-hot coffee. I glimpsed someone in the bushes. Then suddenly they shot at me! The bullet was so close, the sound zinged past my ears. Shaking, I rushed inside. I had not driven my children to school yet, so I huddled them under me in the kitchen. I grabbed the phone on the counter to call the police. My phone was dead. The line had been cut. Frightened they may try to come in, I left my children behind the kitchen counter and I ran to our gun cabinet and pulled out a rifle. Day and night, whoever was in the woods beside my home kept my children and I hostage within my house. Ronnie was on his boat on the coast. The phone line was cut, so I could not call him or the police. We were alone.

When it became night, there was a light shining in the woods. I felt it was taunting me, to let me know they were still there. After two days of my children and I not surfacing, friends and the police came to check on us. No more gunshots had been fired. Also, during the time they held us hostage, they never tried breaking into our home. They must have seen the guns and knew we were hunters. Plus, I slept with the children in my bed and a loaded rifle in my arms to protect us.

Police checked the woods and saw signs of someone being there. They also found the bullet mark on the side of the house but no bullet and no suspects . . . hmmm, no suspects.

If that attempt was by the Vietnamese to kill me or stop my lobbying efforts, it failed. I continued lobbying that legislative session on behalf of the commercial seafood industry. I also shared the truth of the events in Seadrift, Texas, with trusted lobbyists and legislators.

Constantly concerned for my children's safety and my need to feel protected and get a peaceful night's sleep, I often asked my husband to come home. I wanted to rest for a while in his strong arms. However, Ronnie was a hardworking man and an avid hunter, two things that came first in his life. He was not a consoling sort of person. My needs put a strain on his priorities and an additional strain on our collapsing marriage.

In time, where the Vietnamese could not stop me from lobbying, my failed marriage did. Ronnie took the business and I received the best end, our children.

In 1982 Dale's body was discovered; it was two years after his death. He was found on the Aransas Pass Game Preserve near where he and Josie had gone to work running their crab traps. Dale had missing teeth, his lower jawbone was missing, as was a foot. They identified him first through his mailbox key in the pocket of his yellow slicker pants. Josie had been found wearing his slicker coat. Dale's family had his remains cremated.

A PLACE OF REFUGE

In 1980, after Josie and Dale's death, when Mother and Daddy agreed to move to Louisiana, Rudy bought them a small mobile home, believing it was only a temporary place for them to live. However, with no more reported threats, my parents returned to a peaceful fishing and farming existence. Our parents were always grateful for what they had, so they lived contented in that tiny old mobile home for many years.

Mr & Mrs Aplin's Golden "50" Anniversary

In 1994, for their sixtieth anniversary, Noopy gathered private donations from family and friends to surprise our parents with a new mobile home.

Mr. and Mrs. Brawder T. Alpin
60th wedding anniversary
celebrated at G. Chenier
The 60th wedding anniversary   Annie Rupp. Deceased children
of Brawder Thomas Alpin, 77, and   are Billy Joe Alpin and Josephine

Our parents lived in Grand Chenier, Louisiana, until Rudy's untimely death—a heart attack at fifty-five years of age in 1997. The day of Rudy's funeral, through tears, Daddy cried, "I'm tired of burying my children." That night my father died of heart failure . . . or a broken heart.

Mother had now buried her third child and her husband of sixty-three years. Being a lady of faith, she was determined to live and tell others about the love of Jesus. Mother would often say, "If those men had known Jesus, they would have never murdered my son." I of course had never told any family members the truth surrounding Josie and Dale's death. Even though my siblings believed it to be murder, I never confirmed it.

My precious mother passed away in 1999 of an enlarged heart. An enlarged heart effectively described our mother. She was a wonderful, loving lady adored by all who ever knew her. Mother lived an exemplary life by living her faith.

My oldest brother, Doc "Bubby" Aplin, passed away at sixty-eight years of age, also from a heart attack.

Sarah "Noopy" Aplin passed away from a heart attack at eighty years of age due to a doctor withholding her heart and other medications when she was admitted for a kidney infection.

Margarette Aplin spent the rest of her life with mental issues with fear, and died at sixty-seven years of age from cancer. Because of her mental health problems, her reports of hip pain, breast and chest pain, then vomiting with extreme weight loss were basically ignored. She had complained for two years. After Margrette developed a strange cough, they examined her lungs and discovered a tumor the size of a grapefruit and a collapsed lung. Bone and lymphatic cancer were throughout her body. After their diagnosis of cancer, she lived only two months before going onto life support. I was Margrette's medical power of attorney and removed my precious sister from life support on Valentine's Day in 2018. The pain of seeing her appear to strangle to death as they shut her breathing apparatus off has never left my soul.

Zonie Aplin, my fifth-oldest sibling, lives in Florida, where she moved with our mother. After Daddy's death in 1997, Zonie and her husband, J.C. Fruge, moved to Florida so Mother could be near her sisters and several other relatives. Zonie still has a beautiful voice and loves to sing. She is also like Daddy at growing her fresh vegetable garden.

I, Annie, am the youngest of the Aplin children. Soon after my divorce, I became an officer for Hays County Sheriff's Department. In time, I left my employment with the sheriff's department and later worked for a helicopter company in Louisiana. I met and married an ex–Vietnam pilot. We were happily married for twenty-one years before he died of Agent Orange, which was due to his military service in Vietnam. During our marriage, I served as a Christian missionary in countries such as Cuba, Venezuela, China, Jamaica, with my husband in Haiti, and in many other countries. I now live in the mountains of Southern California, where I continue my missionary outreaches in Liberia with standing invitations to Kenya, Nigeria, and India.

Annie at her husbands grave on the island of Maui.

I have also continued being active to wake America up by sharing the truth of the flaws within our country's political system and the various news outlets. When President Trump dared to call out the news for "fake news," we applauded him because it is unfortunately true. Also, when President Trump began requesting that Congress work on our weak and ineffective immigration laws, we again applauded him. In forty-one years, since my brother Billy Joe Aplin's murder, President Trump is the first president I have seen tackle these two destructive entities.

Needless to say, here in California when Kate Steinly's cold-blooded murderer walked away free, my family was not surprised, because it had happened to them.

Billy Joe Aplin

THE END

CPSIA information can be obtained
at www.ICGtesting.com
Printed in the USA
FSHW020656241020

9 781631 296796